UNDERSTANDING
KAREN TEI YAMASHITA

UNDERSTANDING CONTEMPORARY AMERICAN LITERATURE

Matthew J. Bruccoli, Founding Editor

Linda Wagner-Martin, Series Editor

Also of Interest

Understanding Maxine Hong Kingston, Julia H. Lee

Understanding Chang-rae Lee, Amanda M. Page

Understanding David Henry Hwang, William C. Boles

Understanding Gary Shteyngart, Geoff Hamilton

Understanding Gish Jen, Jennifer Ann Ho

Understanding James Baldwin, Marc K. Dudley

Understanding Kazuo Ishiguro, Brian W. Shaffer

Understanding Sharon Olds, Russell Brickey

Understanding William Gibson, Gerald Alva Miller, Jr.

Understanding William H. Gass, H. L. Hix

UNDERSTANDING
KAREN TEI YAMASHITA

Jolie A. Sheffer

THE UNIVERSITY OF
SOUTH CAROLINA PRESS

Published by the University of South Carolina Press
Columbia, South Carolina 29208

www.uscpress.com

Manufactured in the United States of America

29 28 27 26 25 24 23 22 21 20 10 9 8 7 6 5 4 3 2 1

Library of Congress Cataloging-in-Publication Data
can be found at http://catalog.loc.gov/.

ISBN: 978-1-64336-031-7 (hardback)
ISBN: 978-1-64336-032-4 (ebook)

For Daniel and Benjamin

They straddled the line—a slender endless serpent of a line—one peering into a private world of dreams and metaphysics, the other into a public place of politics and power. One peering into a magical world, the other peering into a virtual one. "Will you wait for me on the other side?" she whispered as the line in the dust became again as wide as an entire culture and as deep as the social and economic construct that nobody knew how to change.

Karen Tei Yamashita, *Tropic of Orange*

CONTENTS

SERIES EDITOR'S PREFACE

The Understanding Contemporary American Literature series was founded by the estimable Matthew J. Bruccoli (1931–2008), who envisioned these volumes as guides or companions for students as well as good nonacademic readers, a legacy that will continue as new volumes are developed to fill in gaps among the nearly one hundred series volumes published to date and to embrace a host of new writers only now making their marks on our literature.

As Professor Bruccoli explained in his preface to the volumes he edited, because much influential contemporary literature makes special demands, "the word *understanding* in the titles was chosen deliberately. Many willing readers lack an adequate understanding of how contemporary literature works; that is, of what the author is attempting to express and the means by which it is conveyed." Aimed at fostering this understanding of good literature and good writers, the criticism and analysis in the series provide instruction in how to read certain contemporary writers—explicating their material, language, structures, themes, and perspectives—and facilitate a more profitable experience of the works under discussion.

In the twenty-first century Professor Bruccoli's prescience gives us an avenue to publish expert critiques of significant contemporary American writing. The series continues to map the literary landscape and to provide both instruction and enjoyment. Future volumes will seek to introduce new voices alongside canonized favorites, to chronicle the changing literature of our times, and to remain, as Professor Bruccoli conceived, contemporary in the best sense of the word.

Linda Wagner-Martin, Series Editor

ACKNOWLEDGMENTS

I am grateful to Linda Wagner-Martin for being enthusiastic about the project from the beginning, and to the staff at the University of South Carolina Press for shepherding the book to completion. I first learned about this series from Jennifer Ho, who provided encouragement, advice, and invaluable feedback both early and late in the process. I am also indebted to Julia Lee, Rei Magosaki, Sarah Hagelin, and Bill Albertini for responding to chapters. Their incisive and generous comments enriched my thinking and improved my writing—and reminded me of the pleasures of being part of a robust intellectual community. Lauren O'Connor contributed perspicacious research assistance, for which I am deeply thankful.

I first encountered Karen Tei Yamashita's fiction during graduate school at the University of Virginia, in a course taught by Caroline Rody. I was then, and remain now, awed by Yamashita's inimitable originality, sly humor, and sincere humanism. This volume has been motivated by an effort to find order and patterns in the output of a writer I deeply admire but whose work has frequently overwhelmed and confounded me. I began teaching Yamashita's novels, in part, to better understand them. I want to thank my students at Bowling Green State University who joined me on this journey of exploration, including Najla Alblaimi, Carmen Alvarez, Joshua Catalano, Hannah Espinoza, Lucas Fullenkamp, Susan Howard, Jeena Kim, Michail Markodimitrakis, Clitha Mason, Hannah Maulden, Mitchell Noah, Cody Osterman, Elizabeth Pysarenko, Nichole Rued, Bincy Abdul Samad, Stormy Trotter-Lloyd, Ying-bei Wang Eldridge, Brock Webb, and Daniel L. Williams. To the many students, colleagues, family, and friends who helped me to think through Yamashita's work and write this volume, I offer you my profound thanks; you are my partners in this collaborative endeavor. Over the course of writing this book, my estimation of Yamashita has only grown. I've found myself incredibly moved by her boundless imagination, ethical rigor, clear-eyed wisdom, and guarded optimism. Her work, for all its humor and cynicism, demonstrates the hope that we might yet remake our world to be more just, egalitarian, and sustainable—if only we learn from the lessons of our past. Hers is a voice we desperately ought to heed in these troubled times.

I proposed this volume not long after the birth of my son, Benjamin Ellison, and completed it when he was three years old. His presence shapes every page, for he has given me an entirely new understanding of history, legacy, and intergenerational connection. Words cannot express my gratitude for him, and for Daniel McInnis, without whose love, support, and encouragement none of this would be possible.

CHAPTER 1

Understanding Karen Tei Yamashita

Karen Tei Yamashita is one of the most significant, ambitious, and widely taught contemporary Asian American writers. Her work is invested in the individual and community effects of Japanese internment during World War II and of periods of anti-Asian xenophobia throughout the twentieth century. She has said, "The designation Asian American for me carries a history of solidarity, struggle, and advocacy. The work that this particular American history does is to teach, remind, and to cause change. For example, it's possible through a history of wars, imperialism and colonialism, to trace immigration patterns into the United States."[1] But such national traumas constitute only one element of her capacious imagination, which is equally invested in understanding the movements of people around the world for more than a century. Truly, she is one of the most trenchant and provocative contemporary writers on globalization.

A recurring theme in Yamashita's work is the deracination, or uprooting from a native environment, that international migrants experience while living in countries that are not "home." Treated as strangers in a strange land, these migrants are both hopeful about their futures and frequently feel let down by the realities of their present lives. As experienced by multiple generations of migrants, life is a contradictory mixture of optimism and disappointment, of putting down roots and feeling like perpetual outsiders. In Yamashita's work the Brazilian concept of *saudade* is a particularly apt way to describe these complex and contradictory emotions; as she explains, the term captures "a complicated net of sensations: joy for life, sadness for time passing, hope for the future" (*Circle K Cycles,* 135). Yamashita's writing explores the cultural no-man's-land between countries and cultures. Unlike many other ethnic American writers whose focus is on immigrant assimilation into a new home nation, she instead explores the social limbo experienced by transnational migrants whose identities are cobbled together from repeated journeys and multiple cultures. In this way, Yamashita revises what Sau-ling Wong refers to as the twin tropes of immigrant movement, from movements motivated by economic or political "necessity" to those related to "extravagance" as the ethnic subjects grow more economically and socially comfortable in their new home.[2] In contrast, Yamashita's fictions are populated by transnational migrants who move back and forth between states of relative belonging and stability, rather than following a one-way trajectory toward assimilation and upward mobility.

Given her global canvas, perhaps it makes sense to describe her as her friend and colleague Ryuta Imafuku does, as an "Asian-Anglo-omniphone writer," for her writings are quite distinctive for their movements between three languages—English, Portuguese, and Japanese. Yamashita emphasizes fluidity rather than fluency, highlighting all that can and cannot be translated across languages and cultures.[3] She describes the "struggle with the colonization of language and mind and the difficulty of communicating with our immigrant parents and grandparents—their difficulty in speaking correct English, our difficulty in becoming completely bilingual—and thus to pass on memory and truth."[4] Rather than focusing on a unidirectional flow toward "fluency," Yamashita is interested in the ambivalences of language, how it can be incommensurate or inappropriate, a tool of communication or coercion. The migrant is her paradigmatic subject, one continually on the move and who longs for communication, but is uncertain that language can ever adequately express their thoughts and feelings.

Indeed, Yamashita's characters often cannot or choose not to take root in their transplanted environments, and instead learn to live in liminality. Much of her work explores both the ways people fail (or refuse) to adapt to customs in new lands, and the ways they seek to maintain (or even invent) traditions when they are in a new landscape. For the transnational subject in Yamashita's work, "home" is a complicated term, often triangulated between a land of ethnic roots, a land of educational or economic opportunity, and in-between zones occupied by migrants. When asked in an interview, "Where's home for you?" her answer reflects the value of itinerancy and living in the present: "I like living in Santa Cruz in California. Home is where there's a hot shower."[5] This emphasis on transience is about more than just a kind of bohemian free-spiritedness. Rather, to Yamashita, more fixed notions of home are often an illusion, as her relatives found out when they were interned during World War II or as the long-term residents of San Francisco's International Hotel discovered when they were evicted in 1977; being a citizen or considering yourself a "real" American is no guarantee of safety or security. Better to embrace flux, to be prepared for change. Hers is a world populated by rolling stones who are altered by the different terrains they traverse without being ground down. Her own life provides a model for making a virtue of mobility.

Life and Career

Karen Tei Yamashita was born on January 8, 1951 in Oakland, California. At age one, she moved with her family to Los Angeles county, where she grew up. During her childhood, her father, the Reverend H. John Yamashita, was a minister, and her mother, Asako (née Sakai) was a homemaker. Yamashita grew up with one sister, Jane Tomi, who is two-and-a-half years younger. The family experienced a sudden and dramatic change of circumstances when John had a massive stroke in 1964 and thereafter was forced to retire. At that point, Asako went back to school at the University of Southern California to earn her teaching certificate. She became an elementary school teacher in the Los Angeles Unified School District, where she served for nearly twenty years. This lesson in adapting to new conditions is one Yamashita's parents and grandparents repeatedly learned, and it is a theme she has explored repeatedly in her writings.

Over the course of multiple generations, Yamashita and her family have been forced to adjust to unexpected reversals of roles and prospects. Yamashita's maternal and paternal grandparents were first-generation Japanese Americans (issei) who immigrated to the San Francisco Bay Area around the turn of the twentieth century. Her maternal grandparents Kitaichi Sakai and Tei Imai opened the Uoki Sakai fish market and grocery store in the Japantown neighborhood of San Francisco not long after the 1906 earthquake that devastated the city. Her mother Asako was the fifth of nine children born in the family's home; unusually for the era, she graduated from college, earning a degree in psychology from the University of California, Berkeley in 1941.

Yamashita's paternal grandfather Kishiro Yamashita came to the United States to pay off the family's debts, and he continued to send remittances to his father for the rest of his life. Yamashita's paternal grandmother Tomi Murakami came from a prominent sword-making family in Tokyo. She married Kishiro in Tokyo in 1901, when she was eighteen years old. Tomi and Kishiro opened a tailor shop called Yokohama Tailor Co. in Oakland, catering to the Japanese American community. They eventually had seven children, of whom Yamashita's father, John (Hiroshi), was the fourth. The family grew up in a diverse community with ambitions for upward mobility. As John's sister Kay recalled, "We were not confined to a ghetto situation. All our playmates were non-Japanese. In grammar school, in junior high school there were quite a few Japanese Americans, but not a lot."[6] Six of the seven Yamashita children went to the University of California, Berkeley, including John, who graduated in 1935 with a degree in political science and economics. However, by the time of the Great Depression, Kishiro was in debt, and he died suddenly in 1931. Shortly thereafter, and with John's management assistance and encouragement, Tomi opened Mayfair Cleaners, where she did tailoring and alterations until 1941, when everything changed yet again.

After the bombing of Pearl Harbor in December 1941, the United States declared war on Japan. With Executive Order 9066, dated February 19, 1942, President Franklin Delano Roosevelt effectively declared all U.S. residents and American citizens of Japanese ancestry on the West Coast of the United States (but not in Hawai'i) to be threats to national security.[7] The order authorized the relocation and incarceration of nearly 120,000 Japanese Americans, nearly two-thirds of whom were American citizens and none of whom were ever found guilty of any treasonous acts. The race-based incarceration remains a stain on U.S. history. Thousands of families lost their homes, businesses, and belongings, with little or no compensation. In all, Japanese American families are estimated to have lost more than a billion dollars in wealth and property. Only in 1988 did the U.S. government formally apologize, providing $20,000 in reparations to each survivor; by that time, only 82,219 survivors were alive to collect.

Like thousands of other families, the Yamashitas were first held for several months in hastily adapted horse stalls at Tanforan Racetrack, before being interned in the desert of Topaz, Utah. At the time of his detention, John was youth pastor at the Oakland West Tenth Methodist Church. The Yamashita family remained incarcerated at Topaz until 1943, when John left the camp to attend Garrett Biblical Institute (later renamed Garrett Theological Seminary) in Evanston, Illinois, and his siblings scattered across the country in a series of forced relocations. In his personal and professional life, John was profoundly influenced by Dr. Howard Thurman, who cofounded the integrated Church for the Fellowship of All Peoples in San Francisco in 1944 and whose theology of nonviolence shaped generations of civil rights activists. After the war, John devoted his efforts to rebuilding the Japanese American community in California, continuing to fight for civil rights for all of the nation's citizens, and providing support to immigrants. Yamashita explores the Yamashita family stories of life during and after internment in her memoir *Letters to Memory* (2017).

Yamashita's mother's family were also profoundly shaped by the war and their internment at Topaz. Upon returning to San Francisco after their incarceration, the Sakai family were relieved to discover that their fish market and grocery store, including their delivery truck, were intact, allowing them to reopen the business. Because the family could once again make an income, Yamashita's maternal grandmother Tei Sakai was able to send boxes of packaged food, including baby food, to her sister's family who were struggling to survive in devastated postwar Japan. These family stories of loss, racial injustice, and inequality left a deep impression on Yamashita that is reflected in her various writings.

While the traumas of war and internment indelibly shaped the family, so too did the quotidian and joyful activities of mid-century American life. Yamashita's parents met in 1946, and their first date was a typical postwar college activity: a Cal–Stanford football game. John and Asako shared a social circle, as she was a friend of John's sister, Kay. John was smitten immediately, and soon proposed marriage, but Asako deliberated for more than a year before accepting. They married in 1948. While happily married for nearly four decades, the two were very different temperamentally. Asako "was *unobtrusive,* unpretentious and reserved. John was the storyteller, garrulous, funny, and always entertaining" (*Letters to Memory* 84). Yamashita clearly takes after her father, being a born storyteller with a sharp sense of humor who puts those gifts in service of social justice. But she also has her mother's love of world travel and gift for letting other people steal the spotlight, for Yamashita is rarely a main character in her globe-trotting works but is instead a keen observer of other people, attuned to social mores and distinctive voices.

Yamashita and her sister grew up near the University of Southern California campus. She recalled growing up "in central Los Angeles in a Japanese American community housed inside an African American neighborhood, community, and culture in the 1950s–60s. Many of us L.A. Asians, mostly sansei in the day, were raised on civil rights, soul, and later politically on Malcolm X and the Black Panthers."[8] Much as her father's vocation as a minister was indelibly shaped by internment, Yamashita's novelistic imagination was shaped by the increasing heterogeneity of Los Angeles and the cultural foment of the youth-centered revolutions of the civil rights, black power, Chicano, and yellow power movements.

Encouraged by her parents to learn about another part of the country, Yamashita attended Carleton College in Northfield Minnesota, graduating Phi Beta Kappa with a B.A. in English and Japanese Literature in 1973. At Carleton she studied American literature from Bob Tisdale and cultural anthropology from Paul Riesman. She recalled how these professors "encouraged intellectual query, showed how ideas come about creatively, [and] mentored with integrity."[9] She also recalled being influenced by hearing Alex Haley, the author of *Roots* and Malcolm X's biographer, speak at Carleton about the importance of understanding family history.[10] These lessons would shape her writing career.

Yamashita spent her junior year as an exchange student at Waseda University in Tokyo, where she read Japanese literature in translation and traced her father's family back fourteen generations. She ultimately stayed in Japan for a year and a half, teaching English to raise money for a trip around the world. In *Circle K Cycles,* she describes living in Japan in that period, saying that "As time passed, I exchanged my American clothing for Japanese, grew my hair, got contact lenses, and lost my tan. I also developed an intuitive grasp of mimicry."[11] While she effectively "passed" as Japanese, transforming her body to conform to dominant cultural expectations in Tokyo, her interior experience was more ambivalent. She wrote, "I knew from spending a year in Japan that I was not really Japanese."[12] If her parents learned during World War II that one's physical appearance could be used to justify exclusion, Yamashita learned from her study abroad that looking like one belongs does not guarantee feeling at home.

After graduation from Carleton, Yamashita studied Portuguese, and in 1974 she won a Thomas J. Watson Fellowship, which allowed her to study the history of Japanese immigrant communities in Brazil. With the encouragement of sociologist Maeyama Takashi at the Estudos de Nipo-Brasileiros, Yamashita began recording oral histories of the first generation of Japanese immigrants who had arrived in Brazil as early as 1908. That project soon expanded to include multiple generations of Japanese Brazilians. Yamashita spent nearly three years researching and interviewing dozens of people who were part of the Japanese Brazilian community in the states of Paraná and São Paulo. As she began to shape the material she collected, Yamashita recounts, "I turned to fiction in the form of a novel of historical fiction because I could not see my way to focusing the material into something narrow or specific that an academic work might require."[13] She also attributes her shift to fiction as a practical and ethical consideration based on the limitations of her fluency in Japanese: "I cannot read Japanese. I could do some reading when I was in Japan, but I couldn't keep it up. I was interviewing in Japanese, but mine is not a sophisticated Japanese. Also I couldn't read the newspapers from the period. I couldn't read letters, diaries, or archival materials."[14] While she sometimes jokes that she switched from anthropology to fiction "to avoid having to footnote [her] sources," her work is deeply rigorous in its commitment to truth. As Yamashita explained, "I still adhere to trying to keep the integrity of historic time and place and cultures. I think that intense and thorough research keeps fiction honest. And because of my relationship built over time with real people who live and lived real lives, I feel responsibility to their stories and memories."[15] This sense of responsibility to history, combined with the limitlessness of fiction, has shaped Yamashita's work over four decades and across various genres.

While in Brazil, she met Ronaldo Lopes de Oliveira, a Brazilian architect and artist of Portuguese, Spanish, Italian, Indian, and African descent. They married in 1977 and had two children, a son named Jon and a daughter named

Jane Tei, both of whom were born in São Paulo. Yamashita describes her children as "a bunch of mixed up mutts and mongrels. We call ourselves the Yama-Olives and claim a path back to Africa, indigenous Brazilian Indians, Europeans . . . and yes, Japanese."[16] Lopes de Oliveira has been a creative collaborator for many of Yamashita's works, his observations and flights of fancy providing the impetus for some of her most original stories and novels. As she explained in an interview, "He would make up a story, I would ask him what he thought happened next and we'd go back and forth like that. . . . All of Ronaldo's versions are oral stories, told over dinner usually. I wanted to collect these stories, but I also wanted to change them enough to make them mine."[17] Lopes de Oliveira's history of work with Brazilian theater also provided Yamashita with fodder for explorations into the experimental Los Angeles theater and performance scene.

Yamashita lived in Brazil for a total of nine years before returning to California. Her time in Brazil had a lasting impact on her writing. Her early short stories, poetry, novels, and plays explicitly depict aspects of Brazilian life and Japanese Brazilian community experience. More broadly, Yamashita's peregrinations clearly inform her interest in the transnational movements of people and goods across the globe, as well as her formal experimentalism. She seamlessly incorporates and adapts aspects of Latin American magical realism and telenovelas, along with deep concern for environmental issues such as the destruction of the rain forests. Unlike many other Asian American writers of roughly her generation—figures such as Gish Jen, Jhumpa Lahiri, Chang-rae Lee, and Amy Tan—whose novels usually focus on assimilation within the United States and who write mostly within realist modes of representation, Yamashita depicts characters who are always on the move, unwilling or unable to put down roots in just one place, and she expresses their cultural heterogeneity through experimental forms. (In this way, she has more in common with a writer like Ruth Ozeki, who similarly explores transnational movements and renewed relationships with Japanese culture by Japanese American subjects.)

Yamashita describes herself as "a perpetual foreigner in both America and Japan. Neither by birthright nor blood right do I truly belong in either place."[18] This sense of permanent outsiderness provides her a distinctive vantage point from which to analyze American, Brazilian, and Japanese cultures. Indeed, the more Yamashita traveled, the more confident she felt. She revealed, "I think at the beginning of my travels as a student in Japan, I was quite traumatized by my sense of dislocation and strangeness. Triangulating this experience with a very different sense of reception in Brazil gave me a feeling of strength and self-confidence. I guess over time I learned to travel and finally to feel comfortable in my traveling body."[19] Yamashita's ambivalence becomes profoundly productive when a third culture is involved, moving away from a binary model of communication (fluent/nonfluent) or cultural adaptation (passing/not passing) into something more fluid, asymmetrical, and multitudinous. Both literally and figuratively, Yamashita's fictional worlds seem to be about the uneven and incomplete process of translation—across multiple languages, cultures, feelings, gestures, and genres. This emphasis on translation (with all its imperfections) keeps present the lived experience of language. Language is endlessly adaptable, capable of expressing both the collective and the personal—as well as failing to communicate adequately complex emotional truths. Yamashita expresses "a writerly truth woven around words gathered from reading, from translation, from experience, from memory, but also from words that travel, migrate, immigrate and settle, settle in other places and inside other minds."[20] Instead of feeling constrained by what can't be said due to one's level of language acquisition, her work focuses on what one can say, feel, or imagine in and across distinct languages/cultures. With this model, there is no "right" or "wrong" way to speak, move, or be; there are simply infinite varieties of human experience and expression.

Yamashita began gaining attention by winning several prestigious competitions and fellowships, particularly those for Asian American writers. In 1975 she won first place in the *Rafu Shimpo* Short Story Contest for "Tucano"; she also won first place in the Gremio Literario: Colonia Short Story Contest for her own Portuguese translation of that story. That same year, "The Bath" was published as a contest-winning short story in *Amerasia*. In 1977 she was awarded a Rockefeller Playwright-in-Residence Fellowship at East West Players, which was founded in Los Angeles in 1965 to challenge dominant representations of Asian Americans. Yamashita's play, *Omen: An American Kabuki,* featuring original music by Alan Furutani, premiered at EWP in 1978 under the artistic direction of the Academy Award-nominated actor Mako.[21] In 1979, another short story, "Asaka-no-Miya," won the James Clavell American-Japanese Literary Award, founded by the author of *Shōgun*.

1984 was a watershed year for Yamashita, both personally and professionally. Yamashita, her husband, and children moved from Brazil to Los Angeles county. Yamashita developed "Asaka-No-Miya" into a play; *Hiroshima Tropical,* a work in progress about Japanese Brazilians who believe Japan won World War II, was performed at East West Players. Yamashita ultimately abandoned these theatrical projects, as it was not an opportune time to write about Japanese jingoism around the time of World War II, just as the Japanese American community was deep in conversations with the U.S. government about reparations for internment. For all her outrageousness on the page, Yamashita has always been a politically engaged and ethically motivated writer; she didn't want to distract from (or, at worst, provide ammunition for critics of) the reparations movement. She moved on to other projects that reflected the disorientation of her return to Los Angeles.

The city had been transformed in the time she was gone. In 1984, the Reagan era was well underway and the Olympics put U.S. nationalism on display. Just as dramatically, the city's racial makeup had shifted to include large Latino populations and a significant Korean American community, in addition to long-standing Japanese American, Chinese American, and Black communities. Yamashita's move required an internal, psychological shift to accompany the external changes she observed. As Yamashita describes, "When I decided to return after nine years in Brazil to the U.S., I became not just the wanderer anymore; I became the immigrant. I had to work and support my family in a new country."[22] Needing to earn a living, she got a job at the local PBS station KCET through her sister Jane, who worked in its legal department. Yamashita stayed at the television station for more than thirteen years, working as a secretary to engineers and technicians who set up satellite dishes, microphones, and cameras in the field. She also wrote technical material and managed budgets. She would later incorporate some of these experiences into her novel *Tropic of Orange,* along with her observations about the changing demographics of the city. As she recalled, "I felt a kind of exuberance about this mixed new L.A. community, but in 1992 there was a riot, and it's very sad that we never really resolved any of the problems about race and community or improved our understanding."[23] All of Yamashita's work is about this productive tension between optimism about possibilities for creating inclusive communities and disappointment when those opportunities are missed or squandered.

During the years she worked at KCET, Yamashita continued to write in her spare time across a variety of forms and genres. She wrote short stories, poetry, essays on literature, nonfiction articles about Brazil, and translations of Brazilian journalism and literature for magazines and newspapers, as well as material for multimedia and stage performances. In 1986, she cocreated the short film *Kusei: An Endangered Species* with her husband and Karen Mayeda, who also served as director and producer. She also wrote a number of performance works with the composer Vicki Abe, including *Rock Candy* (1987), a musical about an all-women rock band; *Hannah Kusoh: An American Butoh* (1988), a satirical multimedia examination of stereotypes about Asian American women; and *GiLArex* (originally titled *Godzilla Comes to Little Tokyo,* 1989), which depicts the dangers of gentrification and urban development on the environment. She also wrote an updated, transnational version of Georges Bizet's opera *Carmen* entitled *Tokyo Carmen vs. L.A. Carmen* (1990); and *Noh Bozos: A Circus Performance* (1993), which featured satirical versions of Japanese American celebrities in order to highlight the limited public roles for Asian American men. These performance works demonstrate Yamashita's interest in experimentation and collaboration, as they combine music, dance, videos or slide projections, narration, and dialogue. Many of these theater and performance works were collected in *Anime Wong: Fictions of Performance* (2014), edited by Stephen Hong Sohn, along with several newer pieces.

These early theater works are ruminations and riffs on mainstream stereotypes of Asians and Asian Americans in mass culture, from opera (Giacomo Puccini's *Madama Butterfly,* W. S. Gilbert and Arthur Sullivan's the *Mikado*) to early cinema (Charlie Chan and his Number One Son, Fu Manchu, and Dragon Lady) and late twentieth-century martial arts films (Bruce Lee, *The Karate Kid*). Yamashita's performance works enabled her to begin working through ideas about gender and race that had unsettled her since college. As she recalled of her time at Carleton and Waseda, "Being in Japan had completed a cycle of self-hatred begun in America, my felt alienation within an insolated [sic] and provincial Japanese American community and its cliquish social pecking order, and . . . my prodded sense of foreignness in Midwestern America."[24] These performance works, created in collaboration with other Asian American artists, gave her room to explore the gendered stereotypes of Asian Americans, which have tended to oscillate between "yellow peril" fears and "yellow fever" fetishism, leaving little room for flesh-and-blood human beings. Yamashita's performance work taught her how to expand her repertoire to include nontextual genres like dance and music that would shape her subsequent experimentations in fiction.

In short, Yamashita's works for performance shaped her later narrative work both thematically and formally. With *Through the Arc of the Rain Forest* (1990) Yamashita announced her arrival as a major new voice in English-language literature. Yamashita's singular vision is manifested in her decision to narrate the novel from the point of view of a ping-pong-ball-sized satellite hovering by the head of Kazumasa Ishimaru, a Japanese immigrant to Brazil. Yamashita's cheeky humor and fascination with cultural translation can be seen in the character of Ishimaru, whose name is a reference to the narrator-adventurer-survivor of Herman Melville's *Moby Dick*. Implicitly, the work asks the reader to imagine a late twentieth-century Japanese immigrant to Brazil as a modern-day sailor who is cast about by the maniacal, self-destructive will of global capitalism. The novel was widely hailed for its formal audacity and sharp critique of late twentieth-century global capitalism. The *New York Times* credited Yamashita with skillfully crafting "a parable of ecological devastation that also captures the baroque complexity of Brazilian culture. . . . Ms. Yamashita presents a critique of human waste and stupidity that is fluid and poetic as well as terrifying."[25]

The novel won the Janet Heidinger Kafka Prize for fiction by an American woman as well as an American Book Award from the Before Columbus Foundation, founded by Ishmael Reed to recognize American multicultural literature.

Through the Arc of the Rain Forest was quickly followed by *Brazil-Maru* (1992), a novel about the founding, struggles, and near collapse of a Japanese socialist collective in rural Brazil over the course of the twentieth century. Based on the extensive ethnographic interviews Yamashita conducted with Japanese Brazilians during her Watkins fellowship, and drafted before *Through the Arc of the Rain Forest, Brazil-Maru* is an early experiment in what would become Yamashita's signature polyvocality, with the finished text narrated by five different characters, each of whom provides new information and perspectives on the events discussed. Over the course of many years, Yamashita completely rewrote the novel multiple times to clarify and sharpen its point of view. *Brazil-Maru* continues her exploration of the ways that cultural touchstones and intellectual history canons are reshaped, transformed, and even deformed across space and time; her early twentieth-century Japanese migrants to Brazil draw inspiration from Jean-Jacques Rousseau's European enlightenment classic *Emile, or On Education* (1762) for their own noble experiment to create a new society. *Emile* explores the corrupting effects of society on innately good individuals, offering a vision for humane education and citizenship. But in Yamashita's novel, it is selfish individuals who often corrupt high-minded communities. *Brazil-Maru* was selected by the *Village Voice* as one of the best books of the year. *Kirkus Reviews* described the work as "often seeming more a work of reportage than a novel," but praised Yamashita's creation of "characters [who] are vital, full-bodied creations."[26]

Yamashita's third novel, *Tropic of Orange* (1997), brought her fascination with global migration to North America, reimagining several of the signal events of the 1990s, including the Los Angeles riots, the North American Free Trade Agreement (NAFTA), and political debates about undocumented immigration from Mexico. Following seven characters over seven days as they traverse the Mexico-United States border, *Tropic of Orange* demonstrates Yamashita's restless experimentation with form. The novel's structure was partly inspired by her secretarial work at KCET, for which she created Lotus spreadsheets. She began by "writing a novel in chart form."[27] In his review for the *Village Voice,* Ed Morales praised the novel's depiction of "the economic devastation that NAFTA has wrought on both sides of the border," as well as Yamashita's "poetry, her rich linguistic gymnastics, and her sweetly cynical optimism about human nature."[28] *Tropic of Orange* was a finalist for the Paterson Fiction Prize by the Poetry Center of Paterson, New Jersey, and the novel quickly became a classic on university syllabi. With these successes, Yamashita left the television station to become a full-time writer.

Yamashita has published all of her book-length works with Coffee House Press, a small, independent, nonprofit publisher and arts organization in Minneapolis, Minnesota. CHP was founded by Allan Kornblum, a poet and publisher who was inspired by the small press movement of the 1960s and 1970s that aimed to give voice to writers ignored or marginalized by mainstream publishing. Kornblum was an early champion of Yamashita and encouraged her to send her work to him for publication. Yamashita trusted many of Kornblum's insights as an editor, forging a decades-long partnership. The two shared both literary and political sensibilities in terms of their criticisms of monopoly capitalism. Rei Magosaki notes the parallels between "Yamashita's critique of globalization and Kornblum's own outspokenness about the debilitating competition against major presses housed under conglomerates, often with access to their own distribution networks and possessing enough capital to cut deals with chain bookstores."[29] Even after gaining national recognition for her work, and Kornblum's death in 2014, Yamashita has continued to publish with Coffee House Press.

Yamashita's globe-trotting adventures would come full circle in 1997, when she received a Japan Foundation Fellowship to study the Brazilian community living in Japan. The fellowship, combined with an inheritance from an aunt, allowed Yamashita and her family to relocate to Seto, Japan for six months. During this period, Yamashita contributed monthly travel journal entries about her feelings of dislocation to CafeCreole.net, a multilingual forum moderated by Ryuta Imafuku, Yamashita's sponsor for the Japan Foundation Fellowship. CafeCreole.net is a website devoted to "a new era of hybrid/creole writing with digitally mediated consciousness." *Circle K Cycles* (2001) is the literary product of Yamashita's experience of returning to Japan more than twenty years after studying there during college. *Circle K Cycles* is a hybrid text that intersperses the CafeCreole journal entries with short fiction about the new generation of *dekasegi* workers—Japanese Brazilians recruited to Japan in the 1990s as low-skilled laborers. The result is a kind of travel scrapbook depicting the confusions, complexities, and dislocations of transnational migration. Leo J. Mahoney credits Yamashita for her portrait of a "complex globalized twenty-first-century stew of laboring class migrations, cultural diffusions, and loosening national identities."[30] *Circle K Cycles* serves as the final volume in what might be called a trilogy about Japanese Brazilian migration, which began with *Through the Arc of the Rain Forest*.

That same year, Yamashita was hired to teach creative writing and Asian American literature at the University of California, Santa Cruz. An innovative and committed teacher, Yamashita devotes her time during the academic year to her classes, reserving her writing for summers and research leaves. In 2001 she was named a UC Santa Cruz Distinguished Teacher and in 2009, she received the university's Chancellor's Achievement Award for Diversity in recognition of her mentorship, advocacy, and leadership within Asian American and Pacific Islander studies. A professor of literature and creative writing, she was coholder (with Bettina Aptheker) of the University of California Presidential Chair in Feminist Critical Race and Ethnic Studies from 2012 to 2015.

Yamashita's approach to teaching mirrors her research and creative practices, bringing together wide-angle and close-up views of her subjects. Yamashita recalled one Asian American literature course she taught in a ten-week quarter, for which she put thirty books on the syllabus: ten books of poetry, ten novels, and ten short story collections. Each week Yamashita selected a volume of poetry, a short story collection, and a novel on a particular ethnic group. Students could choose which of the three to read, so that they created their own syllabus within the larger syllabus. The result was a kaleidoscope, where the class as a whole had a large body of work on which to draw, but each student had their own distinctive take on the subject and personalized store of knowledge.[31]

Santa Cruz is a suitably foreign but familiar territory that has been a productive launching pad for Yamashita's literary output. She described the city as "a strange encounter, the crossroads of an old and continuing experiment, vestiges of which abound in evolving and renewed formulations: cooperative life styles, Native and Asian religious and therapeutic practices, an abundance of organic and vegetarian foods, a strong feminist and lesbian community, and likely every martial art and drumming style the world has to offer . . . Students complain that Santa Cruz is a place of appropriations, a gathering of people fascinated with the exotic, usurpers of the culture of others."[32] With its combination of old and new, global and local, authentic and ersatz, Santa Cruz seems a fitting intellectual and creative home base for Yamashita. Her own family and literary archives are housed in the Special Collections and Archives of the McHenry Library at UC Santa Cruz, ensuring the city will continue to be a site of pilgrimage, intellectual exploration, and creative inspiration.

With *I Hotel* (2010), a towering work of historical fiction about the political foment of the years 1968 to 1978, Yamashita's career hit a new peak. The novel depicts the many individuals and community organizations involved in the Asian American movement, with the eponymous International Hotel as its headquarters and spiritual heart. Told over the course of ten novellas, dozens of literary genres, and upward of a hundred characters, *I Hotel* brings to life the mantra that "the personal is political." The novel captures both the promise and the failures of activism during the 1960s and 1970s. It won Yamashita accolades and recognition from new groups of readers. The National Book Award committee named *I Hotel* a finalist for its prestigious award, describing it as "stylistically innovative, vertiginous, and sweeping" and "a miraculous blend of fact and fiction."[33] In 2011 Yamashita was named a USA Ford Fellow by United States Artists, a philanthropic foundation that provides unrestricted $50,000 awards to "America's most accomplished and innovative artists."[34] *I Hotel* also earned the 2010 California Book Award, a Gold Medal in Fiction from the Commonwealth Club of San Francisco, the Asian/Pacific American Librarians Association Award in Fiction, the 2011 Asian American Literary Award and the Asian American Members' Choice Award from the Asian American Writers' Workshop (NY), and the 2012 Association for Asian American Studies Prose Book Award. As Yamashita's work has grown more ambitious, she has become one of the most important literary and political voices in the United States today.

In 2015, Yamashita's mother Asako died at age 98. Yamashita had already become the unofficial Yamashita family historian, collecting her father's and his six siblings' correspondence, photographs, and scrapbooks documenting family members' lives over the previous century. With the death of the last member of the nisei generation, Yamashita began examining these family documents more carefully. *Letters to Memory* (2017) is the result of those explorations. It is an autobiographical work of family history about Japanese internment, as well as an intellectual rumination about the cyclical nature of war, xenophobia, and love. This epistolary memoir is told through a series of one-sided conversations with historical philosophers reimagined in contemporary guises as friends and colleagues.

Writing for the *Boston Globe,* Nina MacLaughlin described *Letters to Memory* as "a challenging, varied work, in moments deeply personal and impressionistic and in moments pulling back into a voice of epic omniscience."[35] With this most recent publication, Yamashita weaves together the themes and formal experiments of her entire career, combining the careful archival exploration and in-depth interviews of *Brazil-Maru,* the autobiographical ruminations on alienation in *Circle K Cycles,* and the genre-busting innovations of *Tropic of Orange* and *I Hotel.* With each new work, Yamashita has grown both more expansive and more interior. As she becomes more formally daring, she simultaneously dives deeper into the personal and familial experiences that have shaped her life and work. The result is a fascinating juxtaposition between the personal and the historical, fact and fiction, memory and imagination, the individual and the collective. Thematically, her work can be understood as an effort to probe the wounds of migration and exile in order to better understand how those experiences shape individuals, communities, and national cultures. Yamashita is distinctive for her deep humanism and humor, as well as a gimlet-eyed view of humankind's capacity for violence, selfishness, and cruelty. As Jinqi Ling aptly describes, Yamashita's "provocative redefinition of the spatial, metaphorical, and linguistic boundaries of Asian American literature has been both enabling and frustrating to her readers across traditional and emerging disciplinary concerns."[36] These contradictions make her a fitting writer for the contemporary period.

Formal and Thematic Patterns

As suggested above, Yamashita's fictions are formally dazzling and original. She particularly rejects the familiar tropes expected of "multicultural writers," such as the *bildung* plot or assimilation-as-cautionary-tale morality play. Instead, her canvas is global, conjuring the unexpected intimacies and distances created by international capitalism, as people and goods traverse continents in asymmetrical circuits. In this she dramatizes the ideas in scholar Lisa Lowe's book *The Intimacies of Four Continents,* which highlights the intertwining of enlightenment idealism and colonial exploitation. Conjoining magical realism and social realist critiques of neoliberal economic policies, environmental catastrophes like the deforestation of the Amazon rainforest, and gentrification in historically ethnic neighborhoods, Yamashita brings a uniquely transnational and contemporary perspective to her portrayal of American preoccupations.

Indeed, her fictions are notable for their refusal to be contained by narrative conventions of identity, point of view, or plot. As noted above, *Through the Arc of the Rainforest* is narrated by a mysterious satellite in front of the head of a Japanese expatriate in Brazil, while *Tropic of Orange* imagines that the latitude line of the Tropic of Cancer is irrevocably pulled northward by an errant citrus fruit. In *I Hotel,* Yamashita effectively gives voice to a building, the late lamented International Hotel, which served as a central symbol and physical hub of the yellow power movement for over a decade. In all of these works, she moves effortlessly between the literal and the figurative, the concrete and the abstract, the particular and the universal. Her novels are polyphonic, prismatic, and perverse, refusing easy synthesis or summarization. She has a profound gift for capturing the distinct voices of diverse characters as they wend their way between global cities such as Los Angeles, Tokyo, and São Paulo. As she explained, "I worked a great deal at creating narrative voices that might capture this rhythmic sound sensibility . . . I also speak Portuguese and some Japanese, and maybe it has to do with having to physically reproduce the cultural attitudes that accompany any language that makes me a bit of mimic. I also wrote for the theater. Paying attention to syntax and speech patterns is maybe something I've absorbed over time."[37] She is also modest, downplaying her ambition and accomplishments.

Yamashita has been described as an "irreverent" writer for her playful experimentation with form. She claims to feel no sense of fidelity to the various genres like magical realism and film noir that inspire her, saying she "ripped them off, parodied, and satirized the genres as useful to the narratives. Maybe writing is an irreverent business by necessity. At the same time, thinking about it, I think I'm pretty reverent about much of what I write."[38] What Yamashita *is* reverent about is the emotional truth of the real people whose stories she mines for her fiction. Having studied anthropology in college and done extensive interviews in Brazil, she takes seriously her obligation to be faithful to the experiences and historical records of those she meticulously researches. As inventive and original as Yamashita is, she grounds her flights of fancy in the quotidian details and psychological complexity of ordinary people's lives. Consequently, she understands her decision to write fiction as "a translation of history and factual events." But she is careful to explain that "fiction is not the same as history. . . . Fiction . . . holds an idea and imagination about history, about time and place and memories, and as such, it is a way to travel into and away from possibility."[39] The process of "translating" history into fiction gives Yamashita room to imagine alternative outcomes that might have been, and in the process to help her readers conceive of futures they might help to create. In contrast to many fiction writers who emphasize their "craft," Yamashita has described her process by saying: "I build a story around ideas."[40] Her novels have indeed centered on Big Ideas, giving her work an intellectual and political spark that is distinctive among her peers. Her work also puts her at odds with many creative writers who operate firmly within the realist mold that dominates most creative writing programs in the United States.

One of the ideas that frequently animates Yamashita's imagination is a deep skepticism of capitalism, whose logic of profit and loss turns human beings into cogs. For example, *Through the Arc of the Rain Forest* tracks the life cycle of a commodity fetish. Her own experience as an administrative wage slave shapes her observations about the alienating and debilitating effects of late twentieth-century technology-enabled capitalism. As she explained, she identifies "with clerical workers, with secretaries." Her short story "The Last Secretary" is "about these limbs, these wrists and hands we use to type, to process words. In fact I was beginning to get carpal tunnel syndrome from typing too much. I began to have an idea that I could be divorced from my digital (as in finger) function and slip into a cyberspace that was [Microsoft] Windows."[41] The shift from the physical world to the disembodied Internet age similarly animates *Tropic of Orange,* with the reporter Gabriel navigating the shift from old-fashioned gumshoe detective work to cybersleuthing.

Yamashita is a both a cynic and an optimist, noting all the ways that people fail to empathize with or understand other humans who are poorer or look different or speak other languages. Similarly, she refuses to simplify minority identities or communities. She destroys stereotypes by showing how multidimensional, contradictory, and paradoxical human beings are. She depicts the twentieth and twenty-first centuries as a Technicolor wonder, full of terrible beauty and tragicomedy, as capitalism's centripetal and centrifugal forces bring people together and throw them apart. Capitalism is the god in the machine, or the Godzilla in the metropolis, driving global transformations. It is creative and destructive. But Yamashita moves beyond hand-wringing, combining her hard-nosed wisdom with a capacious imagination of what might yet be—the multiracial coalitions and multinational communities that could realign the forces of nationalism and capitalism into something more humane, generous, and egalitarian. In her fiction, Yamashita deftly weaves a critique of the inequalities wrought by transnational capitalism with sympathy and humor for those affected. In the words of one of her reviewers, Yamashita's books "carry Heavy Messages. They're crafted, however, not with a sledgehammer but with a wickedly unsettling, iridescent feather."[42] Yamashita herself has described humor and satire as "a kind of daily multiple vitamin for me, and I suppose I learned to take it in Brazil where laughter and joking permeate the culture and reconfigure misery and sadness."[43]

These contradictory qualities make Yamashita a challenging writer for students, but incredibly worthwhile. I vividly recall my first experience reading *Tropic of Orange,* which seemed to short-circuit my capacity for categorization. Similarly, every time I teach *I Hotel,* my students (and I) feel overwhelmed by this massive tome that teems with voices, literary and historical allusions, and genres. Yamashita challenges her readers to learn the complex histories of multiple minority groups and to keep straight a large cast of characters (many of whom are based on real people). But for all its postmodern play with genre, Yamashita's magnum opus reaches out to its readers and demands a response. Students are always eager to discuss this challenging, difficult, but engaging text. Many have deeply empathic reactions to individual chapters and novellas. Such is Yamashita's gift. She makes readers want to better understand the particular histories she directly engages and references. My students want to Google every name and event to learn what is based in real history, to attempt to synthesize this behemoth of a text. Often they cannot tell the difference between the fictional and the historical figures in the book, which is a testament to the ways that Yamashita brings history vividly to life, as well as to how fantastical she shows the past to be. This is equally true of her autobiographical works like *Circle K Cycles* and *Letters to Memory*, which blend fiction and history, autobiography and imagination.

Literary Influences and Legacy

The genre to which Yamashita's work is most often compared is Latin American magical realism. Indeed, Yamashita has confessed to loving the work of Mario Vargas Llosa and Gabriel García Márquez, "who take[s] the bizarre at its face value . . . You take something crazy and make it normal."[44] But she rejects the description of herself as a magical realist writer. Rather, she insists that the fantastical elements in works like *Through the Arc of the Rain Forest* are an accurate reflection of Brazil, which is a nation of contrasts and extremes.

Yamashita also cites Italo Calvino as a literary influence, due to his experimental "storytelling and narrative structures."[45] In her teaching of creative writing, she emphasizes the idea that "more than talent, writing requires a kind of creative, playful, and stubborn resilience." She models this philosophy in her teaching of Calvino's postmodern novel *If on a Winter's Night a Traveler* (1979). Speaking of this work, she explained that it "is a novel explored by 'you' the reader who must navigate the beginnings of ten different novels in which Calvino imitates and reveals the narrative conceits of each novel genre. I use Calvino's novel as a text, parsing out each section into ten weeks, partnering students in panels to present and decipher the work for their fellows, and creating writing prompts to write it yourself . . . What I want to convey is the rich possibility of genre and narrative voice, that no matter what story you tell, you create a character who speaks and imagines for you."[46] Accordingly, Yamashita herself turns to various narrative voices, genres, and styles to reflect the particular stories she seeks to tell. The scrapbook form of *Circle K Cycles* reflects her efforts "linguistically and graphically but also from [her] personal viewpoint, to make the process of writing what might be called a 'fictional ethnography' more transparent."[47] Similarly, Yamashita's early theater work *Hannah Kusoh* relied on the tightly choreographed movements of the Japanese performance tradition *butoh* to underscore her thematic concern with limited roles for Asian American women and the desire to free oneself from such narrow cultural expectations. Rather than operating within a single literary tradition or genealogy, Yamashita is an artistic omnivore who adapts her forms to her subjects. The common denominator among all her works is a sincere commitment to emotional verisimilitude. This is what explains the incredible diversity of forms to which she restlessly turns.

Perhaps due to her penchant for continual reinvention, it is difficult to trace Yamashita's literary ancestors as well as her influence on other writers. Yamashita herself keeps tabs on contemporary writers of Los Angeles, name-dropping the Chicano poet Luis Rodriguez and African American crime writer Gary Phillips in interviews. She has praised Sesshu Foster's poetry and novels, "especially *AtomikAztex*." She noted, "While I grew up in African American/ Japanese American neighborhoods in Central LA and the Westside, Sesshu grew up on the Eastside with the Mexican and Latino folks pressing up against the tracks and the LA River."[48] Yamashita also has expressed admiration for the work of Linh Dinh, Garrett Hongo, Chang-rae Lee, R. Zamora Linmark, Viet Thanh Nguyen, and Hanya Yanagihara. Perhaps her closest literary relatives are other Asian American writers of her generation. These include the poet Marilyn Chin, who moves between languages and cultures to depict (often with a great deal of irony) what it means to be a Chinese American woman; Theresa Hak Kyung Cha, whose avant-garde novels and performance art explore language as a tool of colonization; and Ruth Ozeki, who uses wit and whimsy to explore the intersections of transnational migration and environmental catastrophe. Jessica Hagedorn is another peer who seamlessly moves across genres—from novels to poetry to theatrical performances—and through time and space to reflect the cultural distortions caused by colonialism and globalization. But Yamashita is also connected to younger American writers. In the graphic novels of Adrian Tomine one can hear reverberations of Yamashita's sharp criticisms of the psychological harm caused by popular culture's stereotypes of Asian American men and women. Authors like Jonathan Safran Foer, Hiromi Goto, Larissa Lai, Nam Le, Lisa Ko, Han Ong, Shawna Yang Ryan, and Rakesh Satyal have benefited from Yamashita's genre-busting, polyvocal, global ethnic writing. If she has few direct followers or imitators, that is a testament to her emphasis on individuality and idiosyncrasy.

CHAPTER 2

Brazil-Maru, Through the Arc of the Rain Forest, and *Circle K Cycles*

Yamashita's first two novels, *Through the Arc of the Rain Forest* (1990) and *Brazil-Maru* (1992) feature Japanese characters creating new lives and communities in Brazil. Although published two years later, *Brazil-Maru* was actually drafted before *Through the Arc of the Rain Forest,* during the nine-year period when Yamashita lived in Brazil. Both novels trace the multidirectional flows of goods, people, and ideas from Japan to Brazil (and to a lesser extent the United States), throughout the twentieth century.

Circle K Cycles (2001) is a companion piece exploring the secondary migration of Japanese Brazilian workers to Japan in the 1990s; the work was inspired by Yamashita's return to Japan for six months in 1997 on a Japan Foundation Fellowship. In all three texts, Yamashita reflects on the meanings of concepts like nationality and ethnicity in an increasingly interconnected world, where migration is a condition of existence, whether that be from rural farms to urban factories or across continents. The three works can be read together as a Japanese Brazilian migration trilogy, tracing the transnational movements of people over nearly a century. Yamashita continually questions what it means to be "Japanese" or "Brazilian," suggesting the incredible variability and malleability of culture and identity.

The trilogy is linked by a focus on the intended and unintended effects of globalization on local people, communities, and the land. Over the course of the three books, Yamashita expands her aperture to address larger social forces affecting Japanese people around the world. In *Brazil-Maru,* Yamashita focuses on the familial and quasi-tribal dynamics that threaten to destroy an insular Japanese community in Brazil from within. In *Through the Arc of the Rain*

Forest, Yamashita's players are pawns in an exploitative game of multinational capitalism that threatens lives across the planet. *Circle K Cycles* considers the underground economies and legal no-man's-lands that shape the lives of Japanese Brazilian *dekasegi* (migrant workers) in Japan, where shared ethnic ties are no guarantee of fair treatment or equal opportunity. All three works emphasize how "home" is an increasingly ambivalent and vexed idea.

These texts are populated by a heterogeneous cast of characters, including Japanese immigrants, their Brazil-born offspring, indigenous farmers, ambitious strivers, lost souls, criminals, entrepreneurs, and self-styled shamans. To American readers the story of Japanese "colonies" in Brazil and the movements of subsequent generations might seem like mere historical footnotes. But in Yamashita's hands these stories reveal the legacies of European colonialism, U.S. imperialism, Japanese nationalism, and late-stage capitalism that continue to deepen economic inequality around the world. Perhaps most significant, these three works defamiliarize the twentieth-century immigration story by re-centering it far away from American shores. In this way, Jinqi Ling considers *Brazil-Maru, Through the Arc of the Rain Forest*, and *Circle K Cycles* a trilogy that models an alternative, non-U.S.-centric geography based in Pacific Rim and Chinese-Latin American migration studies. In other words, Yamashita shows readers what global capitalism looks like from other (non-U.S.) vantage points.

Yamashita's Japanese Brazilian novels are also important for giving voice to Asian American studies outside the United States. These texts demand that North American readers critically examine their Euro-American frame of reference, which ignores myriad forms of Asian and Japanese identity across Latin America. Building on her training in anthropology, Yamashita considers how ingrained cultural codes become sites of friction when global economics force diverse peoples to fight over limited resources. She analyzes ethnonationalist cultural practices, such as the foods one eats and how they are prepared, unspoken mores and manners, gender expectations, linguistic nuances, and technology's role in modern life. Such cultural norms are crucial to clear communication, yet they do not translate seamlessly into other languages and locations, creating new barriers to intimacy. The Japanese Brazilian trilogy brilliantly exposes how small such differences really are, yet how profound their effects.

In *Brazil-Maru, Through the Arc of the Rain Forest,* and *Circle K Cycles* Yamashita immerses her readers in the shock of transplantation experienced by individuals or communities putting down roots in new soil. The process of deracination and replanting is fraught with risk and uncertainty. Some shoots thrive in their new environment, others wither, and some become invasive species. These three formally daring novels explore the internal and external factors that shape migrants' responses to their new environments, often with unintended consequences.

History of Japanese Immigration to Brazil and Secondary Migration to Japan

The migration of Japanese workers to the Americas began with the installation of a new Meiji government in 1868. The Meiji period, during which Emperor Meiji ruled until his death in 1912, was distinguished by efforts to make Japan a "modern" nation, which meant ending the policy of isolation that had closed the nation's borders for more than two hundred years. Over the next several decades, Japan rapidly industrialized its economy and increased its role in global trade. By the turn of the century, the nation's focus on urbanization spurred an increasingly neglected rural population to leave the country for greater economic opportunities. The Japanese government encouraged the creation of expatriate communities in foreign countries in the hope of increasing its access to foreign markets.

The first waves of migrants made their way to Hawai'i to work on sugarcane and pineapple plantations, and then to the U.S. mainland to work in agriculture and service industries. However, before long, anti-Asian hostility arose in the United States, first against Chinese contract laborers, and then against the Japanese. The Japanese naval victories against Russia from 1904 to 1905 further inflamed anti-Japanese hostility. In 1907, Japan and the United States signed the Gentlemen's Agreement barring Japanese contract laborers from entering the United States. In the absence of pathways into North America, Japanese immigrants began venturing to South America. The Federal Republic of Brazil, founded in 1889, welcomed Japanese immigration as a means to secure access to Asian markets for its own products. The outbreak of World War I led to a dramatic increase in Japanese migration to Brazil, with most migrants working in the booming coffee industry in São Paulo. By the end of the war, more than 189,000 Japanese had settled in Brazil. Most of these laborers intended to work for a few years, earn money, and return to Japan. But the reality of the plantation economy, with its low pay and scrip system, meant that many had no choice but to stay in Brazil to work off their debts. In addition, the Great Depression and a drought in the 1930s devastated the coffee industry, further reducing opportunities for Japanese migrants to save money for a return trip.

The political climate for Japanese immigrants in Brazil grew markedly worse during World War II, after Brazil sided with the Allies against Japan. Japanese Brazilians were subject to travel restrictions, the confiscation of their businesses, imprisonment, and deportation. *Brazil-Maru* vividly brings to life the experiences of the first several generations of Japanese Brazilians in the first half of the twentieth century, from the early idealism of a socialist colony to the persecution suffered by Japanese immigrants in Brazil during World War II to the fracturing of the Japanese Brazilian community caused by internal divisions. After World War II, Brazil underwent major social and economic changes. In the 1940s less than a third of the nation's inhabitants (forty-one million people) lived in urban areas. Five decades later, more than three quarters of the population (now grown to nearly 150 million people) resided in cities. After several boom decades, the 1980s and 1990s were a period of rampant inflation and slower economic growth.

The Brazilian economic downturn coincided with a shortage of low-wage labor in Japan. In 1990, after three decades of economic growth, Japan began granting visas to nisei and sansei (second- and third-generation) living in other countries to come to Japan to perform unskilled and low-skilled labor. The program coupled economic needs with cultural and racial priorities by privileging ethnically Japanese laborers over other workers, in the belief that these ethnic Japanese would more easily integrate into Japanese life. The new visa program was particularly attractive to Japanese Brazilians struggling with high unemployment. Given the large population of ethnic Japanese in Brazil and Brazil's sluggish economy, the Japanese visa program was effective at recruiting a new labor force to Japan. Within a decade, up to three hundred thousand Japanese Brazilians were living in Japan, working as contract laborers in factories, construction, and service industries. These Japanese Brazilians created new businesses, social service organizations, and community networks in Japan. Many opted to return to Brazil to buy property, while others settled permanently in Japan. For some, however, Japan never felt like home. As of 2016, the Japanese Brazilian community in Japan was estimated at 180,000, while today Brazil is home to the largest Japanese community outside of Japan—more than 1.5 million people of Japanese descent live there. This recent history serves as the springboard for Yamashita's imagination in *Circle K Cycles.*

When read together, Yamashita's Japanese Brazilian novels reveal "the changing positions of economic and political power between Japan, Brazil and the U.S. over time, [and] how technology and capital create degrees of distance and proximity." Just as geopolitical and economic changes affect patterns of migration around the world, technological innovations have profoundly transformed community relations. In short, as Yamashita explained, "The 'trans' in Trans-Pacific or trans-culture used to be over many years and on the opposite side of the globe. Now the 'trans' is a phone call or an email message away. Maybe the 'trans' is what my writing is."[1] With technological innovations, distances can be bridged nearly instantaneously via e-mail or phone call, even as socioeconomic divides grow ever vaster around the world. The Japanese Brazilian fictions explore these shifting relationships, and the costs and benefits of participating in globalization.

Yamashita wrote *Brazil-Maru* first, and it reflects her status as a first-time novelist. In an interview, Yamashita admits that her "second book is really the first."[2] *Brazil-Maru* has a smaller social canvas and a more conventional narrative structure than her later novels. It serves not only as an introduction to Yamashita's writing but also to the history of Japanese Brazilians, as it focuses on the experiences of the first generation of Japanese immigrants to Brazil. In *Brazil-Maru,* Yamashita's trademark polyvocality is present, as is her fascination with the psychological consequences of migration and the dangers of ethnic nationalism.

In *Through the Arc of the Rain Forest,* Yamashita's voice becomes more confident and distinctive and her critique of global capitalism more pointed. She incorporates fantastical elements with an astute ear for speech in order to create a thoroughly original and tragicomic depiction of the devastating effects of urbanization and neocolonial resource extraction on the environment.

Circle K Cycles is the most experimental of the three, creating a collage of autobiography, fiction, advertisements, and found materials to capture the ambivalent experiences of Japanese Brazilians living and working in Japan at the turn of the millennium.

Brazil-Maru

Brazil-Maru began as an ethnographic project. As part of the Thomas J. Watkins fellowship that allowed her to go to Brazil in 1975, Yamashita spent two years interviewing hundreds of Japanese Brazilians to trace the path of immigrant pioneers to São Paulo. She interviewed her subjects in Japanese and Portuguese although she was not fluent in either language, and could not read Japanese. This ethnographic work became the basis of *Brazil-Maru.* Yamashita eventually transformed her notes into a novel written in English, attempting to capture the cadences and phrasings of the interviewees as they were expressed in their native tongues.

When Yamashita arrived in Brazil her focus was on interviewing elderly women who had immigrated from Japan to Brazil between 1908 and 1920. But the men in these women's lives inevitably wanted to add their own versions of the story. Eventually she began interviewing people connected with two Japanese Brazilian farming communes, and she discovered wildly different interpretations of events from each group. This prompted her shift away from scholarly writing and toward fiction. She explained, "I began to see subjects that really interested me: ideas of social systems, use of land, environment, philosophical questions; all of those things came into play. I began to know who these people were in a very different way. If I were to do something more academic, or a sociological study, I would have to prove everything. And I could not do that . . . It had to be fiction."[3] Fiction offered her more leeway to explore and represent the contradictions and emotional truths of the stories she wanted to share.

Yamashita ultimately went through multiple revisions of the novel, completely rewriting the book five times to streamline the story to focus on fewer characters. She later described this process as essential to her development as a writer: "This rewriting was perhaps the beginning of my interest in narrative voice and its complicated possibilities for storytelling . . . It's a subtle task: how to make English look Japanese on the page."[4] To reproduce the voices of the first generation of the fictional community, she relied on her recollections of her paternal grandmother, who came to California from Edo (now Tokyo) at the turn of the twentieth century. As Yamashita explained, "It's possible to say that the characters in *Brazil-Maru* who are presumably Taisho [the era of Emperor Taishō, who ruled from 1912 to 1926] immigrants to Brazil are implanted with the characteristics of a Meiji immigrant to the U.S. as remembered by an American sansei who went to Brazil and interviewed immigrants in broken Japanese and Portuguese and created the final product in English."[5] The novel thus contains multiple translations investigating the dislocations experienced by immigrants across multiple continents, over multiple generations.

In the process of her research, Yamashita learned about small groups of Japanese settlers who emigrated to Brazil in the early twentieth century to create new Japanese colonies based on socialist ideals. Yamashita was fascinated by these stories of idealistic settlers who transformed a wilderness and created new forms of community: "They cut down virgin forests, dug wells, built houses, and planted new fields. The communities that I studied in particular were started by Christian socialists who had ideas of communal and cooperative support systems, following the philosophy of Leo Tolstoy and a Japanese philosopher named Mushanokoji. I was told by the founding issei that they had hoped to create a 'new civilization.' Pretty heady stuff for a student wandering around searching for something."[6] Yamashita shaped these stories into a multi-voiced narrative that captures the hopeful naivete of these early settlers, and how their dreams of equality could disintegrate into infighting, corruption, and greed.

The complexity of human motivation and the difficulties in creating community are reflected in the novel's form, which features five different narrators across as many decades. Yamashita uses Jean-Jacques Rousseau's novel *Emile* as a structuring element (in the form of epigraphs for each section) to highlight how European enlightenment philosophy was a lodestar for many of the communes. But Yamashita complicates the interiority of the European *bildungsroman* with a polyvocality that refuses easy synthesis or homogenization. Each part is narrated by a different member of the community who understands the events and characters in their own way. The result is a novel that accrues complexity with each chapter, casting new light on the events that have come before, and revealing new dimensions to the characters. The novel begins with two families who helped found a new Japanese socialist community in Brazil called Esperança: the Unos and the Teradas. The Unos have four children—the eldest of whom is Kantaro, who becomes the charismatic leader of the group. The Teradas have five sons, including Ichiro, affectionately called Emiru after Jean Jacques Rousseau's Emile. Ichiro is nine years old when the family arrives in Brazil in 1925.

Part I, "Emile," is narrated by Ichiro, who provides the reader's first perspective of the new Japanese farming commune in Brazil. Part I closely follows the *bildungsroman* form, as inflected by a young Japanese immigrant adapting to a new world. Ichiro idolizes Kantaro and is an eager acolyte to his vision of progress. Yet it is the community, not merely Ichiro, that journeys from innocence into experience, beginning full of promise and optimism, but ending with World War II looming, the death of the Terada patriarch, and increasing environmental concerns due to commonplace farming practices.

Part II picks up the story from the perspective of Haru Okumura, the daughter of the group's founding leader and wife of Kantaro Uno. Kantaro and Haru now have five children. The commune seems to be cracking under the weight of its expectations. And the charming, egocentric Kantaro is decidedly less heroic as seen through his wife's eyes. The onset of World War II foments anti-Japanese sentiment across Brazil. Members of the commune are beaten or killed, Japanese-owned business are restricted or confiscated, and internal dissent and rampant sexual abuse against women threaten to tear the commune apart.

In Part III Kantaro narrates after Japan has lost the war. His business dealings regularly bring him to São Paulo, where he builds a second home and a life for himself. He has a lover, Natsuko, a woman who works at a teahouse and whom he has promised a life of ease. Kantaro spends lavish sums out of the community's profits to enrich himself and to fund quixotic experiments.

Back in the commune, Kantaro's behavior both reflects and shapes the behavior of other men in the Japanese commune and in Brazil. His romanticism masks deep selfishness. Kantaro's behavior grows more monstrous, and the commune is increasingly divorced from external reality.[7] Umpei Sawada, a Japanese Brazilian banker, makes huge profits selling yen to those who believe Japan won the war. While Sawada is an opportunist who takes advantage of his co-ethnics, he recognizes Kantaro's egregious mismanagement and wants to hire an outside overseer. But key members of the commune instead ally with the Bahiano, a local Brazilian gangster. The situation grows untenable and, in 1954, Kantaro's commune breaks away with about a hundred followers.

Part IV picks up in 1959 and is narrated by Genji Befu, the Portuguese-speaking nephew of Kantaro. Genji represents the first generation to be born in Brazil and raised in Kantaro's breakaway commune, which is focused on teaching art. Four Japanese artists arrive and fall under Kantaro's spell. Kantaro's wife Haru and his brother Jiro struggle to hold the commune together. Kantaro controls the commune members like a cult leader, preventing young men from growing up, keeping young women under his thumb, and rearranging the community's children into different families. The commune builds a dance stage instead of feeding its members. A visiting artist describes Kantaro's group as "pickled" Japanese—that is, unchanged either by the war or their lives in Brazil (202).[8] As Douglas Sugano explains, "Because he does not remember Japan and because he expresses himself through painting, Genji is the real Rousseauian Emile"—revealing the utopian promise of the colony has collapsed into dystopian reality.[9]

Indeed, the younger generation of Kantaro's colony are all uneducated and/or unbalanced. Genji is increasingly unstable. After a brief sojourn in São Paulo with Guilherme, the assimilated Japanese Brazilian son of Kantaro's friend Shigeshi Kasai, Genji returns to Kantaro's commune. In 1976 one of the commune's benefactors, Shintaro Uguisuyama, invites Kantaro and Genji to inspect land for purchase. The trip is a cover for Uguisuyama to pick up contraband computer chips. Their airplane crashes and only Genji survives, but alone in the forest of Mato Grosso, he loses his mind.

Guilherme narrates a brief epilogue in 1992. He is now a socialist activist married to the Bahiano's daughter Jacira. The two communes have taken very different paths. Kantaro's colony continues to focus on artistic activities, and because their youth receive no formal education, they do not leave. The other commune has pursued agricultural ventures and encouraged its children to go to college; yet its younger generation struggles to find work due to Brazil's weak economy, leading some to go to Japan as *dekasegi*. The story ends with Guilherme learning of Genji's death in the rain forest, an ignoble end to the noble Rousseauian experiment.

Reviews and Scholarship: *Brazil-Maru*

As Pamela Thoma and Min Hyoung Song note, there is little scholarship on *Brazil-Maru,* presumably due its apparent irrelevance to American literary contexts.[10] The Japanese scholar Yukiko Terazawa analyzes collective memory and counter-memory in the novel, but for American readers the activities of a small Japanese commune in Brazil have seemed to be a mere historical footnote far removed from the history of U.S. immigration policy or minority group acculturation.[11] A few exceptions are noteworthy. In her review, Ruth Hsu recognizes that "*Brazil-Maru* depicts the terrible price that we pay when we fail to examine closely heroes or ideals. Although set in Brazil, Yamashita's latest work should cause those of us in North America to reexamine our thinking—for it is Kantaro's 'individualism,' left unchecked by any sense of compassion, family, or responsibility to others that finally destroys Esperança."[12] Kandice Chuh astutely reads this novel as a "hemispheric" text implicitly in dialogue with American-based immigration narratives during the multicultural era. As she explains, Yamashita "reverses the historic-legal exclusion of Japanese from the U.S. literarily, by bringing that narrative to a U.S. readership. Within the context of the cultural nationalist-driven identity movements in the U.S. of the 1980s and 1990s, Yamashita found she was unable to publish work that focused on Japanese in Brazil. Thus, prompted to make the connections that would facilitate U.S. interest in these non-U.S.-based histories and stories, Yamashita establishes these grounds for comparison early on in the novel."[13] The novel periodically reminds readers of the parallels between Japanese migration to the United States and Japanese migration to Brazil, including anti-Japanese racism and internment during World War II. More recently, Nicholas Birns highlights the larger historical context of North and South American settlement, noting that "the community depicted in *Brazil-Maru* would like to have come to the United States, precisely as a consequence of that country's stress on liberty and individuality," but were prevented from doing so due to race-based exclusion acts.[14]

While *Brazil-Maru* invites comparison to United States-based immigration narratives, this does not mean that the story of the Esperança commune functions in merely an analogical or allegorical relation to them. For while Yamashita weaves into her novel patterns of anti-immigration policies and anti-Japanese sentiments that arose across the Americas, she is carefully attuned to the peculiarities of a specific community in a particular time and place. That is to say, Esperança is not a metaphor, but a fully realized place that is shaped by the distinctive features and foibles of its members and their governing principles. As Jinqi Ling describes, "In the end, Esperança becomes a prison house of Kantaro's ideas, while it replicates the ideologies and structures of the modernities it sets out to reject."[15] The novel demonstrates Yamashita's gift for depicting the complexity of individual human behavior and the complications to community ethos occasioned by global migration. This is captured in Kantaro's ruminations on the dreams and failures of the commune: "Although we could not foresee the events of our lives in this world, it is true that we had brought with us everything, all the elements all our cultural baggage, all our wisdom and all our faults, the very impetus to strike out in new directions and all the self-imposed barriers that might deter us from our purpose" (135). This moment of honest evaluation is nevertheless ironic, since Kantaro never admits his particular deficiencies as a leader. Kantaro is a self-deluded egomaniac, but he is not wrong when he says that the seeds of the community's failures came from within. The novel creates a portrait of an entire community that is shaped by a variety of factors: shared "cultural baggage" and individual virtues and vices, as well as external forces (including a world war and various national economic crises). *Brazil-Maru* invites readers to consider the personalities of whole communities—something Yamashita develops on a grander scale in *I Hotel.*

Through the Arc of the Rain Forest

Yamashita considers *Through the Arc of the Rain Forest* a collaboration with her husband Ronaldo; he made up fanciful stories that Yamashita developed into narrative form. As she began writing the book, she would share her ideas with him, and together they would imagine what happened next: "All of Ronaldo's versions are oral stories, told over dinner usually. I wanted to collect these stories, but I also wanted to change them enough to make them mine."[16] Simultaneously an ebullient farce and a thoughtful work of social criticism, the novel takes its form from Brazilian telenovelas. The novel reveals the enmeshment of the poor and indigenous with the operations of global capitalism, mass media, religion, technology, and environmental degradation. A rollicking exploration of the mutual dependence of local and global, the novel underscores the threats to the environment caused by late-stage capitalism.

Formally, the novel demonstrates Yamashita's distinctive voice as a satirist, environmental fabulist, and postmodern multicultural mosaicist. Whereas *Brazil-Maru* focused on one insular, often claustrophobic, Japanese community in Brazil, *Through the Arc of the Rain Forest's* canvas stretches across multiple continents. Divided into four parts, with each part subdivided into chapters told from various characters' perspectives, the novel shows the promises and pitfalls of quick money, media manipulation, and religious fanaticism. These stories converge on the Matacão, a plain of seemingly miraculous magnetic plastic that emerges from the jungle floor. Yamashita's originality is fully manifest with her decision to narrate the story from the perspective of a nonhuman object: a golf ball-sized satellite floating in front of the head of a Japanese immigrant to Brazil. The novel playfully imagines the effects of global movements of people, objects, and capital at every possible scale.

"Part I: The Beginning" establishes characters spread over three continents. Kazumasa Ishimaru (the name is a nod to Ishmael, the exiled narrator of

Herman Melville's *Moby Dick*) is an engineer in Japan with the aforementioned personal satellite before his head.[17] The ball is professionally useful, helping him to identify weaknesses in the national rail system. After privatization costs him his job, he brings his talent to Brazil, where his neighbors are Batista and Tania Aparecida Djapan, a married couple in São Paulo who train carrier pigeons. Mané da Costa Pena is a poor rubber farmer in the Amazon basin who discovers the mysterious Matacão after developers clear-cut the rain forest; he also discovers the healing power of feathers. He meets Chico Paco, a young religious pilgrim who walks barefoot for fifteen hundred miles to the Matacão. After Mané heals Chico Paco's battered feet, Chico Paco builds an altar that becomes a religious destination. In New York City, J. B. Tweep—an efficient, three-armed, but otherwise talentless American businessman[18]—begins to rise through the ranks at GGG, a global multinational corporation seeking economic growth at any cost.

"Part II: The Developing World" shows how the exploitation of Brazil's resources comes at great costs to humans and the environment. The government, the church, businesses, and individuals vie for control of the Matacão. With the help of Batista and Tania's pigeon, Kazumasa wins every lottery he enters and becomes a charitable benefactor. The couple expand their pigeon messenger business, attracting thousands of fortune seekers. When Rubens, the disabled son of Kazumasa's maid Lourdes, miraculously survives an accident, Lourdes writes to the "Angel" Chico Paco, who vows to travel to São Paulo.

In "Part III: More Development," local resources are extracted, packaged, sold, and circulated for the global market. J. B. heads to São Paulo with Michelle Mabelle, a French ornithologist, to figure out how to monetize Mané's feathers, as well as the Matacão plastic. Batista and Tania continue to expand their carrier pigeon business by selling advertising. Meanwhile, due to the smart investment of his lottery winnings, Kazumasa has become the majority shareholder of GGG. J. B. invites Kazumasa to the Matacão under the guise of showing him around the company.

In "Part IV: Loss of Innocence" the boom economy threatens to go bust. J. B.'s third arm seems to wither in the Matacão, while Kazumasa's satellite is ineluctably drawn toward the substance. The media spins increasingly elaborate and inaccurate tales. Chico Paco becomes a radio evangelist, collecting a fortune from devoted listeners. Tania expands the pigeon business internationally. Amid these flows of capital, Lourdes searches for Kazumasa.

"Part V: More Loss" further dramatizes the dangers of overdevelopment. Seeking a monopoly, GGG transforms Matacão plastic into virtually everything: credit cards, no-calorie food, and Chicolándia, an amusement park. Michelle and J. B. become partners in love and business, American capitalism and

European colonialism united for maximum profit. J. B. forces Kazumasa to find new veins of Matacão plastic. But while everyone seems to be making money hand over fist, the migrations caused by the Matacão are harming everyone's relationships and damaging the environment. Then someone kidnaps Lourdes' children, demanding Kazumasa in exchange for their safe return.

"Part VI: Return" demonstrates the human and environmental costs of overdevelopment. A series of feather cultists die after attempting to fly, suggesting dangerous hallucinogenic properties to the plastic feathers. A typhus epidemic threatens to spread globally. During Carnival at the Matacão, Chico Paco is shot and killed. South American terrorist groups murder political dissidents by mimicking Matacão-induced attempts to fly. Batista learns that the typhus epidemic is actually caused by a microorganism on natural feathers; in response, authorities use DDT, which destroys Brazil's bird and livestock populations. Scientists discover that the Matacão is actually ordinary plastic waste excreted by the world's "developed" nations, put under intense pressure beneath the earth's surface, which reemerges in so-called underdeveloped regions. A new strain of bacteria consumes all the Matacão plastic in the world and dissolves Kazumasa's ball. J. B. commits suicide by jumping from the GGG headquarters.

Amid all this death and destruction, there is one happy ending: Kazumasa and Lourdes are reunited and silently confess their love. Kazumasa is transformed, both by the loss of the satellite and by his new familial relationship to Lourdes and her children: he has acquired a "tropical tilt of his head."[19] As Caroline Rody puts it, "the immigrant has become a Brazilian."[20] This happy conclusion, however, comes at the cost of nearly every other character and institution (religion, government, commerce, and media). Following the romantic, individualist logic of the telenovela to its conclusion, Yamashita slyly reminds readers that what might be satisfying narratively is deeply troubling politically. One individual's happiness (or one company's profits) does not undo the sufferings of others. Likewise, Ishimaru's survival, like that of his namesake, was a result of luck more than cunning; the Matacão is a late twentieth-century white whale that destroys the greedy would-be captains of industry who seek to extract its resources. Ishimaru's survival is a discomfiting "happy ending" reminding readers that the good of the many ought to outweigh the benefits of the few, whether those benefits are financial or affective.

Reviews and Scholarship: *Through the Arc of the Rain Forest*

Reception of the novel in the mainstream press was warm, recognizing Yamashita's sharp wit and ecocritical insights. As John R. B. Campbell, in a *New York Times* review, noted, "In this entertaining satire, Ms. Yamashita skillfully weaves [her characters'] stories into a parable of ecological devastation that also captures the baroque complexity of Brazilian culture . . . . Ms. Yamashita presents a critique of human waste and stupidity that is fluid and poetic as well as terrifying."[21] Similarly, in the *Los Angeles Times,* Michael Harris described the novel as "a sermon on the evils of technology worship, media hype, metastasizing capitalism and environmental rape. Fortunately, it's also much more."[22]

Scholarly response has been equally enthusiastic, with the novel being widely taught in college classrooms to demonstrate ecocriticism, postmodernism, Latin American and Asian American studies, magical realism, and Marxian critique of multinational capitalist exploitation. The novel's fantastical elements are widely understood as the vehicle for Yamashita's political message. Thus, Ursula Heise reads *Through the Arc of the Rain Forest* as combining Spanish and Latin American forms with environmental and transnational themes: "Yamashita unfolds a tale whose 'magical realist' turns are designed to explore the ambiguities of an ecologically based sense of place in the age of globalization."[23] According to Jinqi Ling, the melodramatic telenovela plot "effectively dramatizes the magical possibilities of capitalist commercial operations. If soap opera has the tendency to resist narrative closure because of the serial form on which it depends for maximizing such possibilities, then the logic of capitalist operations requires that there be provisional solutions to the periodic crises between capitalism's need for exploration and its tendency to overproduce, due to its overriding concern with profit."[24] In short, the novel's ending suggests just another turn of the capitalist boom-and-bust cycle. Aimee Bahng prefers the term "postcolonial science fiction" to "magical realism" in keeping with her reading of the novel as a parable of neocolonial resource extraction: "Yamashita's *Through the Arc* formulates near-futures that call attention to imperial legacies of exclusion, exploitation, and displacement."[25] Yamashita herself rejects the term "magical realism" to characterize her fiction, instead crediting the fantastical elements of the story to the contradictions inherent in Brazil, "a country that is both developing and developed—and has an Indian and aboriginal culture that is undiscovered and dying. It has an urban culture that is highly cosmopolitan and also very imitative and a government that has pursued policies of bringing this technology into the country. All those things are in this rather strange mix. It's very real."[26] These extremes play out as an exaggerated version of the uneven flows of power, capital, and people that have always been a consequence of globalization.

Yamashita draws explicit connections between colonialism and later neocolonial and neoliberal practices that displace local people and extract resources from the land: "Brazil had once before emptied its wealthy gold mines into the coffers of the Portuguese Crown and consequently financed the Industrial

Revolution in England. This time, if there was any wealth to be had, it had better remain in Brazil. Some scoffed at the pretensions of certain congresspersons, saying that the treasure of the Matacão might, at best, make a small dent in their continuing interest payments to the International Monetary Fund" (96). Yamashita here lays bare the hypocrisies that reinforce and extend the relations of Western European domination into new guises that only further impoverish local Brazilians. *Through the Arc of the Rain Forest* demonstrates the penetration of global forces into even the most remote locations. In Molly Wallace's formulation, Yamashita "highlight[s] the way in which conceptions of the local and national are bound up with global processes."[27] The result is an ever-widening gyre of overdevelopment and underdevelopment, where the short-term benefits of capitalism threaten the long-term health of the world.

Yamashita comically and tragically demonstrates how free market capitalism (abetted by the state) is utterly ruthless, serving to continually increase the gap between rich and poor. GGG's profits never benefit Brazilians, and even Kazumasa's incredible lottery wealth cannot meet the needs of the poor. To the contrary, the lessons of capitalist "branding" spread like a virus, with Kazumasa's supplicants learning to market themselves like products in hopes of being the beneficiaries of his largesse. He laments, "It was a great crime that so many came to swindle a kind man's goodwill, but it was a bigger crime that so many were in so much need" (86–87). Paradoxically—though utterly predictably within capitalism—even as Kazumasa continually tries to gives away his wealth, he accrues ever more capital. Through the sinister magic of investing, money multiplies for the rich while the poor grow more impoverished.

Yamashita also takes aim at capitalism's practice of inventing consumer demand where none existed: "You will recall that before J.B. arrived, GGG had no product on which to test its [marketing] strategy; therefore, GGG developed a strategy that simply created a miracle product that would bring the greatest returns if GGG could control all the markets relating to that product . . . GGG simply produced, controlled and sold everything" (112). With its markets secured, GGG ascribes miraculous medicinal values to the feathers found on the Matacão, complete with advertising: "There was a romantic shot of Mané Pena, the feather guru, walking barefoot across the Matacão at sunset, contemplating this wonderful world and the great mystery of the Amazon Forest. Everything was enveloped in New Age music" (112). GGG's miracle product—the feather—is the ultimate commodity fetish, its market value (and cult value) totally untethered to its use value. In turn, GGG is the ultimate monopoly, without checks to protect humans, animals, or the environment. And the basis for its wealth—the Matacão plastic—is the embodiment of Jean Baudrillard's simulacrum, with capitalism and the media allying to replace the

Real with mass-produced imitations of imitations. Indeed, "the remarkable thing about Matacão plastic was its incredible ability to imitate anything . . . The plastic lily remained the very perfection of nature itself. Matacão plastic managed to recreate the natural glow, moisture, freshness—the very sensation of life" (142). That seductive simulacrum of life, however, is corrosive, eating away at social relations. Wallace reads the novel as a theoretical model of ecocriticism, blending the "Marxist critique of postmodernism offered by [Fredric] Jameson with the kind of interrogation of the nature/culture binary offered by Bruno Latour."[28] Similarly, Begoña Simal, Jesús Benito, and Ana Ma Manzanas describe how the novel "goes beyond the conventional ecological reading not only by questioning the boundaries between natural and non-natural, but also by inflecting the text with a critique of globalized 'logic of late capitalism.'"[29] The novel's ecocritical message is inseparable from its critique of capitalism.

Moreover, the novel shows that even religion, seemingly an antidote to materialism, is prey to capitalism's depredations. Chico Paco begins the novel as a humble pilgrim, offering his thanks for the miraculous recovery of his friend Gilberto with his only valuable possession, his body. Formerly in service to God, he becomes an object of idolatry. As a radio evangelist, he builds a business empire on the prayers of poor souls: "Not only had the pilgrimages become an institution in themselves, Radio Chico was now a bustling entity with new and popular programs, eager sponsors, and thousands of new listeners every day. There were bills to be paid, accounting to oversee, meetings to attend, newsletters to edit, plans to develop. Then, too, there were religious leaders to see or placate, some of them irate, some oozing with religious unction, some looking for an eight o'clock spot. Overnight, Chico Paco was faced with an operation that was bursting at the seams, expanding in every direction without control" (163). Yamashita shows how easily capitalism corrupts religion, transforming selfless prayers for other people into selfishly preying on them. Conversely, Yamashita shows how capitalism takes on the transcendental qualities of religion. Genuine miracles are almost impossible to recognize amid all the ersatz versions for sale. Capitalism perpetually evolves in order to survive, just like a primitive organism.

It is appropriate then that the Matacão meets its match in wild nature. For while humans will willingly sacrifice the long-term health of the entire planet for the short-term economic interests of the privileged few, nature at its most elemental also fights for survival. After the ecological devastation wreaked by humans on the Matacão, humans are in turn decimated by typhus, and Matacão plastic is eaten away by bacteria. Yamashita demonstrates that while humans may imagine themselves at the top of the food chain, nature is relentless in seeking balance.

While the majority of scholarship focuses on Yamashita's treatment of globalization, a smaller contingent of scholars considers the novel's position in Asian American studies. King-Kok Cheung notes that *Through the Arc of the Rain Forest* has been "elided in both ethnic studies and multicultural studies" because it does not "dwell on being Asian or Asian American."[30] Rachel Lee insists that it *is* an Asian American novel, albeit a postnational, transnational one that productively reveals "a fundamental tension involved in interweaving a global thematic with a specific focus on Asian-Pacific and Asian American political concerns."[31] Lee further explains that "Yamashita's novel emphasizes globalization as a multinoded cultural intermingling that is not relayed through the merging of two 'opposites'—for example, Asia and the United States—but through the compilation of heterogeneous national, racial, and cultural components all in one site, the Matacão."[32] The novel's transnationalism forces readers to rearrange entrenched Manichean thinking that compares East and West, global North and global South, to reveal more complex movements of people, ideas, and goods across the globe.

In *Through the Arc of the Rain Forest,* Yamashita explores the idea of the Matacão as a literal magnet embodying globalization, making manifest the many processes that both attract and repel people across the world, and distorting social bonds. Kazumasa's satellite asks sincere questions about the unseen consequences of such a powerful disruption: "What did such an enormous magnet near the equator mean to the Earth? to the Earth's gravitational pull in the solar system? to sunspots? to ecological systems in the forest? to human civilization? to extraterrestrial life in the universe? to the apocalypse?" (98). These questions are not answered, but they haunt the novel. Yamashita returns to the metaphor of the global magnet in *Tropic of Orange.*

Circle K Cycles

While *Brazil-Maru* and *Through the Arc of the Rain Forest* examine the lives of Japanese migrants building communities in Brazil, Yamashita's next book completes the circuit by focusing on Brazil-born Japanese workers who move to Japan. *Circle K Cycles* thus extends Yamashita's interest in transnational movements and diasporic identities through her focus on *dekasegi* in Japan in the early 1990s and 2000s.

The book was inspired by Yamashita's experience living in Japan for six months in 1997. She arrived expecting to develop a historical novel like *Brazil-Maru* but the project evolved differently. She explained that "Japan was in the midst of a violent period while we were there, both domestically, and in other international communities where Japanese were living, too. The Japanese Embassy in Lima, Peru, was being held hostage by a radical guerilla group. . . .

Meanwhile in Kobe, Japan, a series of children were brutally beheaded; their heads were left in front of the school. Within the Japanese Brazilian community, people were having mental breakdowns—a situation serious enough that the Brazilian consulate was conducting an investigative study. Crimes of passion were happening."[33] In trying to capture this strange and unsettling historical moment, Yamashita began collecting material exploring media portrayals of global Japanese identity. What emerged did not fit neatly into a single narrative thread, but rather revealed a series of conflicts and contradictions. As she describes, "I thought I'd get enough material in six months for a novel. But the material was too scattered, not cohesive enough."[34] So she worked the pieces into a collage, extending her writerly project of depicting the myriad forms that Japanese identity takes across the globe through multiple generations of migration.

In *Circle K Cycles* Yamashita alternates autobiographical essays detailing her personal sense of dislocation in Japan with short stories imagining the lives of *dekasegi*. Interwoven throughout the work, the omnipresent Circle K gas station and convenience store reappears as the local hub for all sorts of globalized activity: legal and illegal, comforting and alienating, familiar and strange. The Circle K is a crucial way station for myriad transactions, the place where Yamashita and her fictional *dekasegi* pay bills, park a car, use the telephone, meet friends, or grab a cheap o-bento for lunch. The Circle K, in name and in function, aptly represents the circuits of movement and communications undergirding Japanese Brazilian migrations.

Circle K Cycle opens with a prologue outlining key social and historical contexts of the period. The rest of the book is organized around each month of Yamashita's stay, pairing nonfiction and fiction chapters. The nonfiction essays were written and published on CafeCreole.net during her time in Japan, while the fiction was composed later. In explaining her process Yamashita noted, "There is a kind of writing that can only be produced at the moment and on site. Differently, the 'fiction' for *Circle K* was all written later after returning home, using my notes from my research in Japan. For this book, it seemed to me that the insertion of myself and my family as an understanding or self-critique of the sort of ethnographic work being attempted might be more honest than fiction only."[35] In foregrounding her own positionality in dialogue with the stories she fictionalizes, Yamashita seeks to avoid a kind of queasy voyeurism that might otherwise accompany an imaginative exploration of people who live on the margins of two societies. Befitting such an exploration of cultural liminality, the contrapuntal format of *Circle K Cycles* interweaves fiction and history, autobiography and imagination, the personal and the communal, the particular and the universal. The result is a self-reflective rumination that empathetically imagines a wide variety of experiences.

The first section, "March," uses Yamashita's literal backache as the impetus for a consideration of the ways transportation and communication are the figurative backbone of modern migration. The Internet, telephones, trains, planes, and automobiles provide means of connection, while also offering innumerable opportunities for breakdown. Her short story "Miss Hamamatsu '96" describes a beautiful, young Japanese Brazilian woman who toils at a gray-market job, pirating Brazilian telenovelas to rent to other homesick *dekasegi*. Her boss/boyfriend increasingly takes on the role of manager/pimp, selling her beauty and sexuality. Her dreams of stardom echo those common to the actors in the soap opera plots she copies, but she is far more likely to end up doing pornography or prostitution. The reader observes how easily dreams turn to nightmares in these liminal spaces.

"April" ruminates on differences between Japanese and Brazilian definitions of and attitudes toward "trash." Out of a combination of practicality due to lack of space, economic incentives from the Japanese government, and cultural beliefs, the Japanese throw away many things that are fully functional. The *dekasegi* furnish their homes with these castoffs. In the fiction that accompanies the month's essay, Yamashita illustrates how *dekasegi* are similarly treated as disposable people; Zé Maria Fukuyama describes the labor system as "one mafia," "one great yakuza" connecting the Japanese government, business, finance, the travel industry, telecommunications, and media (33). Collusion among these institutions makes it impossible for *dekasegi* to get accurate information to decide whether to stay in Japan or return to Brazil. The fiction explores just how "dirty, difficult, [and] dangerous" the work available to these migrants is, and how *dekasegi* exist without legal protections from either nation (32).

"May" begins with a collage of scraps of imperfect Japanese English that Yamashita collected from clothing, newspaper articles, job advertisements, and food packaging. These snippets (another kind of detritus) are funny and sad, revealing the desires and disappointments of these foreign-yet-not-foreign workers, including experiences of cultural dislocation, economic and political disenfranchisement, language barriers, homesickness, and destructive coping strategies like drug use. Yamashita follows with an exploration of the Japanese language, which has three different character systems (kanji, hiragana, and katakana), and her own limited knowledge of Japanese, suggesting endless opportunities for miscommunication. The theme of mistranslation continues in the short story "Zero Zero Hum . . . aravilha," which is written in Portuguese and then translated into English (the title becomes "Zero Zero One-derful"). In it, Yamashita unspools various tales of Maria Madalena Oliveira Shinbashi, the woman who defrauded Zé Maria in the April short story and set him up to take the fall for cheating *dekasegi* out of their retirement and health-care funds. Who is this embezzler with multiple aliases? It is impossible to know for sure in this no-man's-land where people can perpetually reinvent themselves and take advantage of newcomers.

In "June" Yamashita considers foods central to Japanese and Brazilian cultures, with their similarities and differences. Language and food both provoke nostalgia, or that which "pleases the literal mother tongue" (83). Her fiction features Iara, a nine-year-old girl who came to Japan at age two to be reunited with her *dekasegi* mother Fátima. Fátima is dating Mário, a fellow Brazilian nisei (second-generation Japanese) who dreams of starting a business with his brother, Sérgio. But Mário has a wife and child in Brazil, and Sérgio is a violent alcoholic. As Iara learns to speak Portuguese, the adults struggle to build lives in Japan, all of them negotiating the pull of the past and the lure of the future. The unanswered question is whether the harsh reality of their present lives will prove to be a worthwhile investment.

"July" outlines the differences between "Japanese Rules," "Brazilian Rules," and "American Rules" for good manners and social mores. Japanese culture privileges order and quiet; Brazilian culture values sociability, gregariousness, and creativity; the United States is defined by cultural imperialism and capitalism. The short story "The Tunnel" continues to follow Fátima and Mário, who are found murdered, their bodies packed into suitcases at the entrance to a tunnel. We hear from Mário's wife Cida and his brother Sergio, who had an affair after Mário left. A phone counselor laments the lack of social services for Portuguese speakers in Japan. We learn that Mário accidentally killed Fátima and was himself then murdered, perhaps by a hit man hired either by his competitor or by a Japanese business partner. The story ends back at the tunnel, where two drivers find two suitcases filled with money—possibly Fátima's or Mário's—which neither driver keeps. The story is convoluted and confusing, revealing the paranoia of those who do not know whom to trust. These "disposable" workers end up as literal trash left by the side of the road, their lives and ambitions wasted.

"August" explores the joys and sorrows of transnational life through Yamashita's diary entries for the 1997 World Cup exhibition soccer match between Japan and Brazil. Yamashita's husband and son meet at the local Circle K to drive to the game with Japanese Brazilian friends. This escapade is followed by an essay on the Brazilian concept of *saudade,* which Yamashita describes in *Through the Arc of the Rain Forest* as "the bittersweet sensation of exuberant but temporary joy" (174). This quintessentially Brazilian feeling has elements of nostalgia, homesickness, and anticipatory melancholy: "Here in the ephemeral present resides a complicated net of sensations: joy for life, sadness for time passing, hope for the future. Saudaude" (*Circle K Cycles,* 135). Because of secondary migration, *saudade* has become an authentically Japanese cultural phenomenon. The month concludes with brief stories about three different couples. Marcolina, a Brazilian woman who is an avowed Japanophile, moves to Japan with Paulo, a Japanese Brazilian; Paulo dreams of returning to Brazil, but Marcolina feels at home in Japan. Mariko and João, both Nikkei (Japanese ethnics in the diaspora), are drawn to each other by their shared sense of limbo in Japan.[36] Marcos Kubo is a Nikkei who falls in love with Yoko, a "mattakunihonjin," one entirely Japanese. While attending a Brazilian Japanese festival, each couple debates the meaning(s) of authentic Japaneseness.

In an epilogue, Yamashita discusses her own bloodline, which indicates she is "a mattaku *complete* Nikkei," though her hair and eyes provoke Japanese interlocutors to assume she is "a hybrid" (145). She ruminates on what Japaneseness consists of, how it is measured—is it defined by blood, culture, geography, language, or phenotype? What do these terms mean in a global world where multiple migrations and intermarriage are commonplace? The book ends with questions, rather than answers, befitting an exploration of the unmooring of identity from any simple equation of geography with ethnicity.

Reviews and Scholarship: *Circle K Cycles*

Reception for this work has emphasized Yamashita's deft exploration of diasporic identities. Leo J. Mahoney, writing for the *Multicultural Review,* credited Yamashita for her portrait of a "complex globalized twenty-first-century stew of laboring class migrations, cultural diffusions, and loosening national identities."[37] In *Contemporary Fiction,* Jason Picone suggested that "*Circle K Cycles*'s brilliant fusing of forms is perfectly suited to its subject matter, giving insight into the kaleidoscopic lives of *dekasegi.*"[38] *Publisher's Weekly* praised how Yamashita "brings it all together with humor and heart."[39]

Academic scholarship tends to focus on the work's formal qualities in relation to themes of nationalism and capitalism. Jinqi Ling reads *Circle K Cycles*'s patchwork format as a visual reminder of the incommensurability of Japanese and Brazilian cultures; Ling explains that "the coexistence of multiple cultures, as visualized in the book . . . is inherently hierarchical and exclusionary."[40] Nathan Ragain connects the short story cycle to economic conditions and nationalism, arguing that "in *Circle K Cycles,* both Brazilian and Japanese national identities are given a material grounding inextricable from the circuit of production, consumption, and the state."[41] Most provocatively, Kandice Chuh considers *Circle K Cycles* to be emblematic of a hemispheric approach to literary studies that rejects any binary geographic orientation. Chuh examines how Yamashita's fictions "reject the progression–orientation of a world mapped in two dimensions (the flat world of modernity that bifurcates neatly into north and south, east and west, modern and not). Instead, they demarcate a circum-oceanic spatial logic characterized by cyclicality and infinite connectivity."[42] The work's form is a vehicle for its theme: *dekasegi* possess no singular, coherent, or cohesive identity, but experience a fragmentary existence at the intersections of multiple cultures and are enmeshed in global economic forces and political alliances.

Brazil-Maru, Through the Arc of the Rain Forest, and *Circle K Cycles* share a fascination with the similarities and differences among national cultures. In *Brazil-Maru,* the Japanese newcomers marvel at differences between themselves and their Brazilian neighbors, seeking to maintain their ethnic identity at all costs. In *Through the Arc of the Rain Forest,* the narrating satellite compares Japan, Brazil, and the United States, noting how "unlike Japan, Brazil was massive, inefficient, encumbered by bureaucracy, graft and poverty. Kazumasa took me, his precision ball, into this tropical and elusive mess like a beachcomber with a metal detector on Coney Island on the Fourth of July" (10). Such passages combine straightforward comparison (Japan vs. Brazil) with simile (the American treasure hunter in high summer at a tourist destination), suggesting continual acts of translation among countries and cultures. Elsewhere in that novel the reader encounters the limits of such comparisons, as the American business GGG selectively appropriates Japanese business practices: "Recycling productive personnel was part of GGG's interpretation of the old courses in Japanese corporate business sense" (53). In *Circle K Cycles* Yamashita more fully explores the idea of cultural translation when she directly compares social mores (around food, trash, and personal comportment) in each nation, accompanied by literal translations of Japanese and Brazilian Portuguese text into American English. Visually, the reader observes the incommensurability of each language, and readers are forced to confront their own ignorance of or lack of fluency in other languages—and, by extension, other cultures.

All three works are further linked by their exploration of the disappointments of modern life, particularly in relation to ideas of technological or developmental "progress." In *Through the Arc of the Rain Forest,* Mané Pena experiences incredible technological "progress" in one lifetime, but at tremendous personal cost: "Once, Mané Pena had been a rubber tapper in the forest, then a simple farmer on infertile soil. Then he had been a mason on construction sites along the Matacão. Now he had left the labor of his former days for a different kind of toil. He had to be places at a specific time. He had to get on airplanes to get there. He had to squint into bright lights. He had to talk about the same things over and over. The stress and tension of this new life was a constant challenge to the effectiveness of the feather" (121). For all its amenities, modern life is lonely and alienated—in terms of both labor and community. Batista laments, "Thanks to Tania Aparecida, they were an international communications system, but being able to communicate for free with Tania Aparecida over thousands of miles seemed a lousy trade-off to having her right there in bed with him" (171). Presaging the debates of the millennial generation, Yamashita shows how technological advancements designed to facilitate communication across vast distances in fact weaken social ties among families and local communities.

Across her Japanese Brazilian trilogy, Yamashita deftly explores the ways that media—whether letters and propaganda sent from Japan after World War II, messages and advertisements carried by pigeons, telenovelas, or pornography—can weaken or distort the bonds of society. In this, her work feels deeply prescient about twenty-first century anxieties about social media's effects on community ties. Yamashita's migrants endlessly seek connections with "home," even as modern technology seems only to create greater psychic distances. Thus, while illegally reproducing Brazilian telenovelas onto VHS tapes, Miss Hamamatsu '96 thinks, "Home was a copy of a copy of a copy of a copy, further away than she could imagine" (*Circle K Cycles,* 20). The very attempt to maintain ties to home can have an attenuating effect, further increasing one's sense of loss. In a similar fashion, ethnic/cultural identity is continually transformed through each process of migration, becoming something new and almost unrecognizable. If the members of the Esperança Japanese commune were "pickled" in *Brazil-Maru,* in *Circle K Cycles* the *dekasegi* feel like they are losing their identities altogether, for they are neither Japanese nor Brazilian, but something new. Yamashita shows us that identity is neither fixed nor capable of being preserved, but is a porous, ever-changing thing.

Another theme that connects these three works is the social construction of gender, which is detrimental to both men and women. Patriarchal norms demanding the submission of women structure Japanese, Brazilian, and Euro-American cultures alike, but women are especially vulnerable to abuse by men whose own social positions are precarious due to racism and poverty. In *Brazil-Maru* Kantaro Uno grows increasingly monstrous in his exertion of power, physically abusing the women who keep the commune (and his second life in São Paulo) running. His behavior grows worse as his mismanagement threatens his control over the commune, and it spreads like a virus among the men. In

Through the Arc of the Rain Forest, Tania Aparecida has a talent for business that had been underdeveloped for most of her life due to the gendered expectations of Brazilian culture and her husband Batista's possessive jealousy. But once the opportunity arose, "Tania Aparecida discovered that she liked to haggle over prices, to make deals and even watch the inflation index. Compared to washing clothing, cooking and sewing, this was so much better" (92). Her success is predicated on increasing geographical distance from her husband (and from Brazilian cultural norms), suggesting a painful trade-off between individual success and community cohesion, particularly for women. In *Circle K Cycles* Yamashita shows how the liminal space of the *dekasegi* creates new opportunities for ambitious men and women to reinvent themselves and achieve their dreams, but often at the cost of new immigrants who are even more vulnerable. Thus, Jorginho pimps out Miss Hamamatsu for increasingly exploitative sexual labor, while Maria Madalena steals from Zé Maria and the *dekasegi* workers whose financial accounts they manage. Yamashita further explores socially constructed gender norms in *Anime Wong: Fictions of Performance* (2014), demonstrating the ways they are reshaped in North America, and in turn how these social expectations constrict women and men from self-expression and connection.

CHAPTER 3

Tropic of Orange

Published in 1997, *Tropic of Orange* marks Yamashita's mature voice and vision on full display. Unlike her previous two novels that were set in Brazil, *Tropic of Orange* focuses on the enmeshment of the United States in global trade and transnational migration and its unanticipated environmental consequences. Yamashita's novel highlights the innumerable connections linking the global North and South, suddenly made visible during a cataclysmic event. Yamashita describes having "written the book in response to a very narrow vision of Los Angeles as Hollywood and a racially divided city between blacks and whites." Returning to Los Angeles after nearly a decade in Brazil, Yamashita was both delighted and disoriented by the changes that had occurred. She explained, "I found a city that was very different, filled with people from all over the globe. I found living here very exciting. I reveled in being here again. I started to take a look at the literature of Los Angeles, but no one was talking yet about that change."[1] In *Tropic of Orange,* Yamashita depicts a city that is diverse both ethnically and economically, but is experienced quite differently by its various communities. As she explained, "the city is a layered geography traversed and negotiated every day differently by different people, and those layers may merge or be distinct yet also represent the city."[2] Rather like Jorge Borges's short story "On Exactitude in Science," Yamashita explores a world whose contours shift in response to the ever-changing imaginary maps that people carry in their heads.

As with *Through the Arc of the Rain Forest,* Yamashita credits her husband for the conceit that animates *Tropic of Orange.* As she explains, "The idea belongs to my husband, Ronaldo Lopes de Oliveira, who had suggested a short story about an orange with the Tropic of Capricorn growing through it.

The Tropic of Capricorn runs through São Paulo, Brazil, where we lived . . . which, similar to L.A., is a techno-industrial mega-metropolis of migrating people. Since we were living in L.A., I asked if I could move the orange to the northern hemisphere and then discovered that the Tropic of Cancer runs through Mazatlán in Mexico."[3] This seed grew into a short story entitled "The Orange," published in the *Los Angeles Times* in 1991. Told from the point of view of a Mexican American teenager in Los Angeles who is the cousin of the Gabriel who features prominently in the novel, "The Orange" begins with "an aberrant orange" growing too early in the season as a result of global warming. As it grows, it pulls the Tropic of Cancer with it, "reverberat[ing] down that imaginary line like sound down the string of a bass fiddle," scrambling ethnic identities, foodways, languages, and class positions around the world.[4] Then, the day after the summer solstice, the orange falls from the tree and rolls down a hill; an unsuspecting farmer picks it up and brings it to the marketplace, where he gives it to a migrant worker headed to California. With each movement of the orange, the geography further distorts, pulling Central America into Mexico. Indeed, "It seemed to [Gabriel] that Panama, Guatemala, El Salvador and the whole rest of Central America were getting wedged up into Mexico. That would be the only explanation for the strange dialects of Indian and Spanish popping up all around him. Also, the weather was heating up; the Equator was moving his way."[5] The story is resolved when the narrator tracks down the orange in Los Angeles and returns it to Gabriel's farm in Mazatlán, where it eventually rots and returns to the earth. Order is seemingly restored by the orange's homecoming to the land on which it was grown.

Yamashita continued to develop this story, expanding and reworking it over the next five or six years into a full-length novel. Instead of the Orange being an unnatural phenomenon directly caused by climate change, in *Tropic of Orange,* global economics catalyze the action, as exemplified by the 1994 North American Free Trade Agreement (NAFTA) that linked the United States, Canada, and Mexico into a single, unrestricted economic market "of almost 400 million people with $6.5 trillion worth of goods and services annually."[6] In the novel Yamashita considers the complex interrelationships between economics, the environment, and society. Whereas some ecocritical writers celebrate wild nature untouched by human hands, *Tropic of Orange* focuses on technology-enabled late-stage capitalism's deleterious effects on both human communities and the natural environment. As ever, Yamashita's environmental consciousness is deeply concerned with human beings.

In both versions, the titular fruit is itself a North American subject buffeted by external forces. It has no agency of its own, but merely reflects the changing territory of the human world. In "The Orange," those forces are man-made effects on the environment; in *Tropic of Orange,* Yamashita emphasizes the unintended consequences of shifting economic and political boundaries. At the novel's beginning, the orange falls off Gabriel's tree, where it rolls "in dusty turbulence down a small slope, under the barbed-wire fence, and just beyond the frontiers of Gabriel's property to a neutral place between ownership and the highway" (13). The novel's orange embodies the dirt, uncertainty, and danger of the liminal space between public and private that migrants perpetually traverse. The orange waits in its no-man's-land, until a local woman carries it to the marketplace, where it begins its journey northward.

Historical Contexts

NAFTA, which went into effect in January 1994, was sold on the promise that it would create jobs in the United States by limiting trade restrictions across national borders. By most accounts, NAFTA primarily helped corporations become more efficient, which resulted in job losses across North America. U.S. manufacturing lost tens of thousands of jobs, while millions of low-skilled Mexican workers were unemployed, accelerating trends that had already begun due to globalization. Indeed, NAFTA, like other neoliberal policies, has probably increased economic inequality by "allow[ing] for larger conglomerates to increase their productivity, [while] it limits the exports from cities and towns built on factories, mills, etc."[7] As an example of the absurdity of contemporary trade policy, Yamashita has one character explain to another that it is actually cheaper to buy a Mexican-made toilet in Los Angeles than in Mexico.

The economic justifications for NAFTA were accompanied by anti-immigration rhetoric, promising that the law would help to reduce illegal immigration by encouraging the employment of workers within each home country. If NAFTA did what its proponents suggested it would do, then low-skilled workers would no longer need to cross national borders to find jobs. However, this promise was always speculative at best, and the last several decades have shown that undocumented migration continued to rise well into the twenty-first century. The divides between rich and poor, global and local, the United States and Mexico are embodied in *Tropic of Orange* by the struggle between the well-equipped SUPERNAFTA and the handmade and homely El Gran Mojado. Their wrestling match is described as "El Contrato con América," echoing Newt Gingrich's 1994 congressional election promise that the Republican Party's "Contract with America" would reduce the size and scope of the federal government. With these flourishes, Yamashita makes clear how politics is a theatrical and spectacular battle of ideas with calamitous material, environmental, and human consequences.

A 2014 report from the Sierra Club and other North American nongovernmental organizations documented the detrimental environmental impacts of NAFTA over the previous two decades.[8] In Mexico, large factory farms that relied heavily on pesticides replaced small family farms with more sustainable practices, and increased mining created industrial pollution. In Canada, NAFTA ensured contracts with the United States for petroleum, resulting in expensive and dirty tar sands operations in Alberta. In the United States, NAFTA resulted in increased pollution, particularly from the Mexican trucking industry, which has laxer air quality standards. According to Ilana Solomon, director of the Sierra Club's Responsible Trade Program, "NAFTA led to an expansion of deforestation and unsustainable water use in order to support export-oriented agriculture. It gave massive rights to corporations to challenge environmental and climate safeguards in private trade tribunals. It expanded exports in dirty fossil fuels in a time when we should be moving beyond these outdated fuels and investing in clean energy."[9] As she did in *Through the Arc of the Rain Forest,* in *Tropic of Orange* Yamashita demonstrates the environmental effects of neoliberal economic policies, and their disproportionate impacts on poor, minority, and politically disenfranchised communities.

While NAFTA operated at national and international levels, the state of California was the front line for many of these debates about economics and politics. In November 1994, California legislators submitted Proposition 187 as a ballot initiative. Emphasizing the financial impact of providing social services to more than a million undocumented immigrants, Prop 187 created a state database to screen for citizenship. The bill allowed citizens to directly report the undocumented to the Immigration and Naturalization Service (INS); the bill also allowed local municipalities to refuse medical treatment, social services, and public education to those who could not prove their status. Republican governor of California Pete Wilson campaigned for reelection by supporting the bill, while President Bill Clinton argued that it would interfere with federal immigration policy. California voters approved Prop 187 by a wide margin (59 percent to 41 percent), largely along political party lines. Lawsuits were immediately filed to stop the law's implementation and a month after Prop 187 was passed, a judge issued a permanent injunction prohibiting the implementation of most of its provisions. In 1997, the law was found unconstitutional because it circumvented federal law. At that point the law was effectively dead, although it was not fully repealed until 2014. Although the law was not enforced, it became a lightning rod both for those who were pro-immigrant and those who were anti-immigrant.

With her depiction of the Harbor Freeway collapse as transportation catastrophe, Yamashita took elements of the Northridge earthquake of January 1994 and the Los Angeles riots of 1992. The earthquake collapsed several California highways and caused up to forty billion dollars in damages in the San Fernando Valley to the northwest of Los Angeles, closing down highways for months. The riots, which lasted six days in April 1992, have loomed larger in the national imagination. They were set off by the acquittal of four white Los Angeles police officers who were charged with the brutal beating of black motorist Rodney King. Just as King's beating had been caught on film—which was endlessly replayed on television in the days leading up to the trial—a local news crew in a helicopter filmed an attack on white truck driver Reginald Denny, who was almost beaten to death by four black rioters. Denny was rescued by black and Latino residents who witnessed the event on live television. Fidel Lopez, a Guatemalan immigrant, was also pulled from his car and beaten by rioters before being rescued by Bennie Newton, a black minister who, decades before, had served time in prison for armed robbery, drug possession, and other crimes. During the week of the riots, television news continuously circulated images of assaults, arson, and the looting of local businesses, mostly in South Central Los Angeles. The total property damage was estimated at a billion dollars, and sixty-three people died (including ten killed by law enforcement or the military). For many Angelenos, the riots were a collective expression of rage and frustration at long-standing police violence, economic racism, and political disenfranchisement directed at communities of color. For some viewers, particularly white, middle-class people getting their information solely from the television, the riots marked the failure of liberal politics, including affirmative action and multiculturalism. In depicting a Los Angeles paralyzed by disaster but whose citizens actually work together to create a new and more egalitarian society, Yamashita reimagines the riots as a peaceful revolution. Buzzworm, the novel's self-proclaimed "angel of mercy," represents redemption in and of Los Angeles as modeled by Reverend Newton.

The events of the novel are also shaped by the infamous televised chase of athlete/actor/accused murderer O. J. Simpson in June 1994, in his white Ford Bronco. With more than a dozen police cars following him, Simpson drove at low speeds throughout the city for more than two hours. This bizarre media event, which captured the attention of millions of viewers across the country, also seized Yamashita's imagination. She recounts these highly mediated moments as a kind of peculiar, hive-mind experience for those living in Los Angeles: "There was this conversation between the media (what was happening on television) and this physical event. There was an uncanny sense that the City had a 'brain,' or collective understanding."[10] In *Tropic of Orange* this kind of collectivity develops when one of the major arteries of the city is gridlocked. In the absence of routinized and racially segregated movements through the city, L.A.'s denizens develop new coalitions and modes of communication.

The novel's experimental shape (seven characters over seven days) was in part inspired by Yamashita's process of learning to create Lotus spreadsheets during her time as a secretary at a public television station. She began by "writing a novel in chart form," plotting out the movements of her characters across time and space. As Yamashita explained, "Writing a novel is a huge puzzle, and I wanted to create some kind of cohesiveness so that I could get through the puzzle . . . I had to work every day as a secretary, and I didn't have time. It's efficient, right? If it's chapter three, this is what's happening. It doesn't work exactly like that because things change as you write, but I tried to stick to it, because it was useful."[11] Demonstrating the increasing narrative complexity of her fiction as well as her efforts to aid readers in navigating her imaginary worlds, Yamashita included not only a table of contents but also the original "HyperContexts" page she created to track each character across each day, through relevant chapters. Ever attuned to technologies' effects on human relationships, the novel thus both alludes to and mimics the forms of connectivity made possible with the rise of the Internet and cable television. Ultimately the novel emphasizes the human costs of treating people like numbers whose only value is monetary. Combined with the fanciful premise that the Tropic of Cancer is physically tied to a single orange, Yamashita makes vivid how globalization and its enabling technologies transform spatial and psychic geographies.

The novel is told from the points of view of seven main characters, each of whom represents a major racial or ethnic group in Los Angeles. As Yamashita readily admitted, the main characters "all started as 'types,' even as caricatures, in the same way the media represents us."[12] Mass media flattens characterizations of minorities, reducing human complexity to familiar stereotypes. But Yamashita subverts those stereotypes, often to highly comic effect, creating a narrative centered on people of color, who are usually relegated to sidekicks or background figures in mainstream narratives. The result is a polyphony of heterogeneous voices, echoing different racial and ethnic histories and demonstrating the complex human consequences of migration.

In *Tropic of Orange* everyone is a transplant from somewhere else, with multifaceted identities shaped by globalization, colonization, and war. Just as the orange that grows from Gabriel's tree was brought to Mexico from Riverside, California and is of a type first imported from Brazil in the late nineteenth century and then grafted into a new species, Yamashita's characters have been shaped by many generations of movement and mixture. Gabriel and Buzzworm show a fascination with transplantation; Gabriel is continually planting fruit trees that seem ill suited to the climate of Mazatlán, while Buzzworm waxes poetic about the palm trees planted along the L.A. freeway. This idea of transplantation is made grotesquely literal with the traffic of human organs, suggesting that many of the dislocations wrought by globalization benefit the wealthy of the Global North at the expense of the poor of the Global South. Under unchecked capitalism, people are turned into goods that can be bought and sold, just like fruit or consumer products.

Formally, the novel is similarly multifaceted and far ranging, alternating among seven different character voices. As Yamashita explained: "Formally, I tried to structure the book as a symphony, where movements or certain instruments come into play."[13] These different voices sometimes come together in glorious harmony and other times threaten to dissolve into dissonance. Along with the different character voices, the novel blends together different literary genres, with elements of the detective novel, magical realism, folk mythology, poetry, and political satire. As Yamashita noted, "There is literary entertainment —magical realism, noir; performance—dramatic and musical; the media—television, radio, and news; the newest toy entertainment—the internet; and finally, the movies—kung fu, Bruce Lee, and Jackie Chan."[14] These genres are inextricably linked to the novel's locus of Los Angeles, entertainment capital of North America and much of the world. Just as agricultural products and people continually travel across national borders, so does culture.

The Novel

The events of chapters one through seven occur on Monday, June 21st, the summer solstice, and introduce the major characters in this multicultural world that seems to grow ever smaller and more interconnected. Rafaela Cortes is an undocumented Mexican woman with "soft Afro-Mayan features" who is separated from her husband, Bobby Ngu, who arrived in the United States as a child after his mother died and his father's bicycle factory in Singapore went bust. Bobby's story provides another vantage point in the narrative of work being outsourced and performed offshore. Such a narrative usually emphasizes the devastating effects to U.S. manufacturing in rust-belt cities; Yamashita instead highlights the economic impact of globalization on small business owners around the world who cannot compete with multinational corporations. Bobby and his little brother have no legal recourse or route into the United States despite the fact that their family's economic plight is intimately tied to American economic practices, so they pose as Vietnamese refugees seeking asylum in the wake of the Vietnam War. Due to the chaos of war and resettlement, and the presumption that all Asian kids look pretty much alike, they are allowed to make their way to the United States. Bobby is another L.A. hybrid, a "Chinese from Singapore with a Vietnam name speaking like a Mexican living in Koreatown."[15] Rafaela and Bobby are struggling to achieve the American Dream, with Bobby starting a cleaning business (among other less legal ventures) and Rafaela working toward a college degree. Rafaela is currently hiding out with their son Sol (a signature bit of wordplay on sun/son) in Mazatlán, Mexico, keeping house for Gabriel Balboa, a Chicano journalist in L.A. who fantasizes about retiring to his Mexican hacienda on the Tropic of Cancer, surrounded by fruit trees from across the globe (7). While Rafaela ruminates on reuniting with Bobby, Gabriel daydreams about Rafaela, imagining himself as a white knight rescuing her from a life of toil. With these details, Yamashita highlights the fact that white savior fantasies are as much a matter of socioeconomic privilege as of race.

In Los Angeles, Gabriel's on-again-off-again girlfriend Emi is an unsentimental, hard-nosed Japanese American television news producer with a penchant for publicly making anti-multicultural statements and mocking white urbanites' faux cultural sensitivity. Buzzworm is a seven-foot tall African American veteran of the Vietnam War with a Walkman radio on his belt and half a dozen watches on his wrists, each one "a story" of someone loved who is now gone (29). A former drug addict, he now serves as the self-proclaimed "Angel of Mercy" and unofficial social worker to the city's homeless. He is also an informant to Gabriel, providing crucial intelligence on the city's underclasses, including Manzanar Murakami, a homeless Asian American man who stands on a highway overpass "conducting" the music of L.A., making his own map of urban movement through sound. Manzanar first appeared in Yamashita's stage musical *GiLArex* (1989). Since that play had a short theatrical life, Yamashita "wanted to resurrect this character" for the novel, where he represents an alternative to the capitalist order of conspicuous consumption, material accumulation, and the relentless pursuit of "progress."[16] Manzanar, Buzzworm, and the marginal communities in which they circulate have long been ignored by government institutions. In the absence of social services, they create their own networks for communication and resource redistribution. Yamashita thus makes clear that globalization devastates the land and further impoverishes the world's poor, creating a vicious cycle of overdevelopment and underdevelopment.

Back in Mazatlán, Arcangel is a wizened, scarred, but wiry "actor and prankster, mimic and comic, freak, a one man circus act" (47) with mysterious holes in his sides, whose poems and performances recounting centuries of colonialism, despotism, and capitalism in the Americas might be genuine miracles. He awakens from a dream that sets him on a journey following "an indefinable point on his visual horizon" (51). Arcangel is a pan-Latin American figure, based on the Mexican American performance artist Guillermo Gomez-Peña and the Chilean poet Pablo Neruda; he represents Latin American history, politics, mythology, and art. According to Yamashita, "Arcangel's performance is grotesque, freakish, yet Christ-like, accounting for 500 years of history in the Americas . . . He takes the poetry, and also the political conscience and history across the border."[17] The novel's first day ends with the previously stable geography of the Americas moving, as an orange growing at the center of the Tropic of Cancer on Gabriel's land falls from its tree and is picked up and taken to a marketplace to begin its journey northward toward Los Angeles. This special Orange moves the Tropic with it, transforming time and space in its path. The Orange is pulled along by the invisible hand of capitalism, with unanticipated consequences for the people and lands it crosses.

On Tuesday morning Manzanar witnesses and mentally "records" in his mind a terrible car accident on the Harbor Freeway in Los Angeles: a Porsche careens into a propane tanker truck, resulting in a hundred-car pileup. Emi arrives with the *NewsNow* van to film the wreckage but leaves to pick up Gabriel after his car breaks down, giving him a ride to the airport where he is meeting a source for a story. Like the hard-boiled detectives he adores in film and fiction, Gabriel is the first person to recognize something strange is in the air. "Something's wrong today," he explains. "I mean the length of the day. The weather. The light for godssake. Time. It's got something to do with time. Place" (61). Meanwhile, Rafaela puzzles over finding crabs crawling around Gabriel's house in their landlocked part of Mazatlán. The very geography is shifting, stretching in unprecedented ways as the Tropic of Cancer begins to move off its latitude. Arcangel follows the mysterious Orange, using his own body to tow a broken-down truck to the marketplace, before heading north with the fruit ensconced in his suitcase.

In L.A. Bobby reads a letter from an unknown cousin requesting money to help her enter the United States. This prompts his memory of how he first met Rafaela a decade earlier, when he helped her illegally cross the border. Bobby is one of the millions of migrants who work endlessly in low-skilled and no-skilled jobs, hustling to make money and stockpiling material goods. Rafaela had grown tired of Bobby's diatribes and the political scapegoating of immigrants as bottom-feeders and welfare queens, so that is why she left her husband and the United States for Gabriel's fantasy of an oasis in the desert.

Buzzworm contemplates the geography of L.A., and what the maps of sociologists and economists can and cannot capture about the realities of a place. While city planners dream of urban redevelopment and revitalization projects designed to bring about gentrification, Buzzworm has his own dream of "self-gentrification by a self-made set of standards and respectability. Do-it-yourself gentrification. Latinos had this word, *gente.* Something translated like *us.* Like *folks.* That sort of gente-fication" (83). On his rounds among the street sellers, a woman sells him an orange from Florida, highlighting the artificiality of official cartographies that designate produce from a thousand miles away as "domestic" while nearby goods from Mexico are "imported." Meanwhile, a child who escapes a gang shooting describes the bullets as seeming to curve in slow motion. Buzzworm gives the kid his orange, before continuing on his rounds through the city.

Emi brings Gabriel to the international terminal of the airport to meet a mysterious Mexican source Buzzworm told him to find; the two find themselves investigating child organ transplant smuggling, which is apparently on the rise as a result of NAFTA. In addition, Emi learns that the freeway accident from earlier in the day resulted in an explosion that destroyed an overpass. The surviving passenger in the original car accident reports that the crash was caused when the driver ate an orange and lost consciousness.

On Wednesday, Bobby arrives in L.A.'s Chinatown to meet the smuggler bringing his cousin. He negotiates the ransom to meet the girl the next day in Tijuana. Buzzworm learns of the mysterious overdose deaths of two different people who were eating oranges, including the young man who saw the bullets curve. Gabriel interviews Manzanar Murakami, who is "the first sansei born in captivity" during the U.S. government's internment of Japanese nationals and Japanese American citizens during World War II. Manzanar graduated from UCLA and became a surgeon before abandoning it all to conduct highway traffic. He does not appear to be mentally ill, but rather seems to have figured out the secret meaning of life.

With the overpass collapsed and the pileup on the freeway, a second semi explodes. The freeway becomes a mile-long parking lot. Manzanar conducts the chaos, as the city's underclasses appropriate the vehicles into a new form of tent city. Food and drinks from abandoned trucks are shared among the denizens, creating a cacophony of car alarms, sirens, and "festive shopping and looting. It was one of those happy riots" (122). Emi and Gabriel watch the chaos on television as they eat sushi at a local restaurant. Emi is more enraged by the white patron who claims "to adore Japanese culture" than by the conditions that allow all of them such comfort and ease while parts of Los Angeles burn. Yamashita thus satirizes both the fetishization of multiculturalism and the hypocrisy of its skeptics.

In Mazatlán, Rafaela talks to her neighbor Doña Maria, whose son Hernando brought some strange oranges from Brazil. Hernando is also involved in the trafficking of child organs for transplants, which makes Rafaela fear for Sol's safety. Later that day Arcangel, on his journey north, transforms into El

Gran Mojado, "part superhero, part professional wrestler, part Subcomandante Marcos. Ski mask in camouflage nylon, blue cape with the magic image of Guadalupe in an aura of gold feathers and blood roses, leopard bicycle tights and blue boots" (132). Now inhabiting the role of a Lucha Libre-style wrestler representing the scrappy ingenuity of the Mexican migrant, Arcangel/El Gran Mojado challenges SUPERNAFTA, the embodiment of American capitalism, to a death match.

The next day, Thursday, time seems to be out of joint, with watches stopping and radio stations stuck. The news reports that oranges have been tainted with cocaine, resulting in two deaths and three hospitalizations. As the police attempt to confiscate all of the city's oranges, residents scramble to find some of the illicit fruit. Arcangel, in the guise of a day laborer, helps out on Gabriel's farm in Mazatlán. Rafaela grabs Sol and a cooler (filled with an illegally harvested organ) that she stole from Hernando. She telephones Gabriel to tell him that she is sending him the cooler so that he can investigate. Arcangel, wrapped in the threads of the Tropic of Cancer, heads north, transforming the geography with every step. Archangel, Rafaela, and Sol take a bus to the Mexico-United States border.

On the freeway, people have created an encampment out of the abandoned cars, "creating a community out of a traffic jam. There's already names to the lanes, like streets! South Fast Lane and North Fast Lane. Limousine Way—that's the off-ramp at Fifth" (156–157). A new society is being created out of the wreckage of the old, with less waste and inequality. Emi sees the endless news broadcasts of the freeway reorganization as a kind of reality television entertainment. Gabriel investigates the tainted oranges, which were smuggled into the United States by C. Juárez, the mysterious woman Gabriel has been following since Monday; he heads to Mexico City to untangle the conspiracy, planning to check on Rafaela along the way. He calls Bobby, who leaves to find his wife and son. Gabriel asks Emi to take over reporting on Manzanar and to look out for Rafaela's package while he is in Mexico.

On Friday, day four of the event, oranges have been confiscated across the city. Emi is designated on-site producer of the news coverage of the freeway reorganization. Buzzworm has taken over as on-air reporter, and he and his homeless friends are doing interviews with gang members and providing tips on urban gardening. The redistribution of the city's resources apparently has beneficial social and environmental consequences. But before long, Emi has advertising and sponsors to monetize Buzzworm's underground journalism, suggesting the gravitational pull of capitalism upon everything. Emi reveals that Manazanar is her grandfather, suggesting the lasting trauma of Japanese internment and the dangers of community silence and amnesia about this history.

Rafaela, Sol, and Arcangel travel by bus to Los Angeles, but the trip seems endless. As they ride, crowds of people follow in anticipation of the match between El Gran Mojado and SUPERNAFTA. While at a rest stop, a villain in a black Jaguar kidnaps Rafaela; Arcangel looks after Sol for the rest of the bus ride north. When the bus breaks down, Arcangel pulls it across the border, along with a hundred thousand laborers who lost their jobs as a result of trade policy. In Mexico City Gabriel meets with his contact, who provides him with computer disks containing information about all the people who have been disappeared in a single village; by phone, Emi tells him how to post the data online. Gabe tells Emi to give Rafaela's package to Buzzworm. In Tijuana Bobby pays the ransom for his cousin, gives her a makeover to look like an American kid, and easily walks her across the border into the United States. In L.A., Manzanar conducts the "the greatest [traffic] jam session the world had ever known" (207). These improvisational encounters run counter to any official policy or pathway.

The next day, Saturday, Arcangel and the crowd of migrants arrive in L.A. Arcangel recalls events throughout history in the Americas and performs more miracles and magic, culminating in juggling the last orange in the city, the magical Tropic of Orange. Buzzworm brings Rafaela's package to Manzanar, who confirms there is an infant heart inside. Down on the freeway, a new kind of normal has settled in, with the homeless making improvements to cars they occupy and creating social services DIY-style. Los Angeles, the quintessential driving city, has become a pedestrian-only zone. On television, national and city leaders create media spin, agreeing to meet to talk about solutions to the city's social problems without making commitments. Buzzworm encounters Arcangel and Sol, creating a diversion to distract the crowd from Sol, who now has the Orange; the crowd follows Buzzworm, and he throws the transplant cooler, like a football, to a receiver who takes off running.

Rafaela fights her kidnapper (Hernando), and the two seemingly transform into the mythic Mexican figures of jaguar and snake. Their battle replays centuries of war and sex between Spanish (and later American) colonizers and indigenous peoples in the Americas, but Yamashita reconfigures and distorts those symbols to reflect the globalized confusions wrought by the Orange. The jaguar—ancient, mythic, and honorable symbol of Mexico—becomes a Mexican drug smuggler and organ trafficker in a fancy imported Jaguar car. In turn the snake, a treacherous figure on the Mexican flag and its coat of arms, is metamorphosed into a mother nobly defending her child. Everything is topsy-turvy, and the literal and figurative become hopelessly entangled. Rafaela awakens bloodied and nearly naked, with a wad of fur in her mouth and a severed ear in her hands. Gabriel recognizes Rafaela by the roadside and helps her to his home. Rafaela asks him to find Sol, who will be with Arcangel at the wrestling match on Sunday. Gabriel comes to the realization that his feelings about the Mazatlán house and Rafaela are nothing but the romantic fancies of a colonialist American man. He goes to Donã Maria's house to use her phone, where he sees a mysterious "X" moving around downtown L.A. on her television. Apparently, the movements of the Orange have made it possible for her satellite dish to register signals previously hidden from public view. On Hernando's desk, Gabriel finds a travel itinerary for C. Juárez. With these new clues, the journalist-cum-detective heads back to L.A.

Bobby brings his cousin home, where he notices that the languages on the television channels are all switched around. He heads to the Ultimate Wrestling Championship to find Sol. Meanwhile, Manzanar is now joined by other homeless conductors and musicians across the city, creating "a kind of choral babel" to welcome Arcangel and the migrants (239). This scene of calm is broken by a single gunshot, aimed at the satellite antenna of the news van, which hits Emi; the source of that bullet remains a mystery, but in response, military helicopters immediately begin shooting at the denizens of the freeway. As seems so typical of governmental reactions to small-scale challenges to the political-capitalist order, a single act of disobedience sets off a disproportionate, unfocused, and militarized response.

On Sunday, Gabriel continues to track the movements of both the child organ trafficker Corazon Juárez and the tainted oranges, which apparently traveled from Brazil through various central American countries in order to traffic drugs under cover of legal trade. On Doña Maria's television, there are now at least ten maps, signaling international crime syndicates tracking their illicit merchandise via global positioning satellites. Gabe posts his findings to the web, where netizens trace myriad conspiracies. Emi dies in Buzzworm's arms. Manzanar recognizes her as his granddaughter and goes with her body as it is lifted into the *NewsNow* helicopter. Emi has become precisely the kind of sensational news story she used to chase, her image circulating on an endless loop on television. Unlike the homeless whose deaths will be ignored, "no one would forget her ultimate sacrifice" (253). As if choreographed by an unseen hand, all the airbags in the city burst simultaneously, "like white poppies in sudden bloom," temporarily stopping the murder and mayhem (258). The population comes together in this moment of other-worldly peace that "had a spiritual quality, like a near-death experience" causing everyone, briefly, to stop and recognize each other's humanity (265).

But this moment of harmony is accompanied by more sinister signs. As Buzzworm walks through the wreckage on the freeway, including body bags lined up in rows (a consequence of the militarized response), he sees some of the homeless people roasting the illegally traded infant organs over a fire; they have effectively (and grotesquely) recycled those human body parts, which were turned into commodities by gangsters, transforming them back into sustenance for human beings. One group of poor people (the homeless) literally cannibalizes other poor people (third-world babies), suggesting the social Darwinist perversions of capitalism. Buzzworm goes home, his radio now only picking up love songs. He turns it off and gives away all his watches when he decides that "solar-powered, he could not run out of time" (267). In giving away these objects, he finally casts off capitalist modes of temporality, seeking a new (though actually quite old) way of measuring his days and remembering his stories. Like Arcangel and Manzanar, Buzzworm is now poised to experience movement through time in nonlinear and non-"productive" ways that offer new knowledge.

Rafaela wakes up at Doña Maria's house, and begins walking to find Sol. On the way, she encounters Bobby. At the Ultimate Wrestling Championship, held at the Pacific Rim Auditorium—a reminder of international alliances and global capitalist arrangements other than those that characterize North America—El Gran Mojado and SUPERNAFTA meet, embodying local vs. global, human rights vs. multinational corporate interests, third world vs. first world, homespun vs. technocratic. Bobby finds Sol and the Orange. Rafaela cuts up the orange and feeds it to Arcangel, while Bobby holds on to the threads of the Tropic. SUPERNAFTA implodes, and Arcangel is mortally wounded, the crowd picking him up to bury him back in Mazátlan beneath the orange tree. After sacrificing his life for the poor people of the third world in the Americas, the Christ-figure Arcangel is brought back to the Tropic of Cancer, where his body will return to the earth. Yamashita makes no promises of resurrection. The novel ends with Bobby releasing the threads of the Tropic in order to embrace his family. In this way, local ties of family and community (and the value of self-sacrifice) seem to conquer the global forces of capitalism, but the victory is temporary, fragile, and comes at great human cost.

Reviews and Scholarship: *Tropic of Orange*

Upon its publication, the novel was recognized in the mainstream press for its imaginative and humane treatment of the effects of international trade policy in the 1990s. In his review for the *Village Voice,* Ed Morales praised the novel's depiction of "the economic devastation that NAFTA has wrought on both sides of the border," as well as Yamashita's "poetry, her rich linguistic gymnastics, and her sweetly cynical optimism about human nature."[18] Writing for the *Nation,* Molly Rauch noted how "Yamashita presents her politics using cartoonlike superheroes and snappy slogans. She also has a cultural historian's refined perspective."[19] These critics recognized Yamashita's marriage of art and ideas, balancing exaggeration and subtlety, comedy and tragedy. Janet Kaye, writing for the *New York Times,* voiced a note of dissent, writing that Yamashita's novel "disappoints as it heads for the home stretch, when her playful seriousness too often gives way to pedantic polemics."[20] As is often the case, Yamashita's politically engaged literature turned off some readers unsettled by her uncomfortable marriage of imaginative storytelling and ideological critique.

These same qualities make the novel a favorite of academic readers, who tend to focus on *Tropic of Orange*'s genre-busting form that merges social realism and science fiction. Sherryl Vint argues that "by using non-realist elements in the narrative, Yamashita makes visible the degree to which the taken-for-granted contemporary LA . . . is itself already science-fictional."[21] The novel's innovative challenge to linear notions of time and space echoes what journalist Thomas Friedman has referred to as the flattening of the world due to globalization. However, where Friedman celebrates this new world order as leveling the playing field among global actors, Yamashita trenchantly emphasizes globalization's role in increasing inequality.

As she makes visible in *Tropic of Orange,* the familiar arrangements of time and space regularized under Fordist and Taylorist modes of production are in the process of being reshaped by the new global economic order. Time and space become distorted when companies can do business across three continents and twelve time zones simultaneously. In the novel, the music of the global city of Los Angeles is heard only by Manzanar, a dropout of conventional society and an invisible person in status-obsessed La La Land, who sensitively recognizes the changing tempo and shifting geography that go unnoticed by most people. Similarly, Buzzworm is like Charon guiding souls to Hades, leading Gabriel through the underworld of Los Angeles inhabited by all of those ignored by, or outside of, consumer capitalism: the homeless, migrant workers, gang members, and other underclasses. Buzzworm contemplates the unmapped, perhaps unmappable, layers of the city in a direct rebuke to the modernist impulse to define and regulate human chaos into neat grids and graphs. In contrast, Emi represents contemporary media's role in flattening human lives into mere sound bites and "cut-tos," all in the relentless quest for profit.

Yamashita's novel demonstrates the idea that global power is increasingly exerted and expressed through economic flows rather than political boundaries. Molly Wallace explains that "consumerism, in *Tropic of Orange,* replaces nationalism as a form of 'postnational' identification that can be exported around the world."[22] Elisabeth Mermann-Jozwiak similarly emphasizes the deterritorialization made possible by globalization, with Los Angeles functioning as "a symbol of the post-national space: it is not a clearly demarcated or homogeneous structure made up of assimilated or assimilating immigrants."[23] For Joseph Entin, Yamashita's novel is less an exploration of postmodern and post-structuralist epistemologies than a reminder of the afterlives of older forms of capitalism; he considers *Tropic of Orange* to be a "labor novel" that "implies that contemporary, cosmopolitan Los Angeles rests on a foundation of colonial and postcolonial labor."[24] In this way, *Tropic of Orange* is both futuristic and deeply historical, as it shares with twentieth-century novels like Frank Norris's *The Octopus: A Story of California* (1901) and Upton Sinclair's *The Jungle* (1906) deep concerns about the dangers of unregulated capitalism to human beings and the environment, while also attending to the distinctive consequences of twenty-first-century policies and technologies.

Tropic of Orange's thematic concerns about globalization's effects on space and time are inextricably linked to its formal experimentation. Rachel Adams characterized the novel as "an afterword to literary postmodernism" that captures "the globalization of American literature."[25] Ruth Hsu summed up the novel as a work that apotheosizes Yamashita's fascination with point of view, suggesting that "*Tropic of Orange* works out most fully a recurrent topic in Karen Tei Yamashita's novels: that there are many truths or experiences of reality."[26] In a related way, Rei Magosaki read the novel as teaching new kinds of reading designed to counteract the forces of globalized postmodernity: "the multiple strands of the novel coalesce . . . when readers learn to shift their attention away from the characters in the center to those in the margins, and notice the world to be populated by the silent laboring bodies of migrants and the dispossessed."[27] These scholars all emphasize the ways that Yamashita invents new literary forms to help defamiliarize, and thereby challenge, the political-economic forms that dominate contemporary life.

The novel's critique of globalization is entwined with its depictions of what Lisa Lowe described as the "heterogeneity, hybridity, and multiplicity" of Asian America, as shown in characters like Emi, Manzanar, and Bobby.[28] Yamashita evokes familiar stereotypes only to shatter them with psychological and sociological complexity. None of them fit the "model minority myth," just as Rafaela confounds the media characterization of the "illegal immigrant," and Buzzworm cannot be reducible to the category of "ex-con." In particular, *Tropic of Orange* is also notable as an Asian American novel that considers the often unspoken, yet long-lasting effects of Japanese internment during World War II on Asian American families and communities. Emi is the novel's cynical, sharp-witted, high-tech digital native who is at home setting up satellite equipment, editing news content on the fly, and navigating dark-web Internet forums. Yet she cannot bring herself even to talk to Manzanar, her own grandfather, who survived internment, became a successful surgeon, and then dropped out of his upwardly mobile life to become a homeless highway conductor. This is no mere generation gap common to many ethnic narratives; this is a traumatic rupture caused by external, institutional forces—not unlike those that label human beings "illegals" or disproportionately incarcerate minority communities over fears of innate criminality. Emi and Manzanar's estrangement is made more poignant by Yamashita's refusal of a feel-good resolution. The family is only reunited when Emi dies and Manzanar accompanies her body in a helicopter, suggesting that traumatic histories can create insoluble ruptures within minority communities.

The novel's treatment of Asian American history is also related to its environmental message. Chiyo Crawford argues that gardening functions in the novel as a tool of resistance linking the history of Japanese internment to modern urban agriculture and climate change; she credits Yamashita with "mak[ing] clear that the battle against environmental degradation demands a comprehensive, humanistic approach that recognizes the lasting effects of race-based environmental inequality."[29] As in *Through the Arc of the Rain Forest,* Yamashita warns of the environmental impacts and unintended consequences (social, as well as ecological) of unfettered "development." But *Tropic of Orange* also presents anti-capitalist modes of living as forms of environmental and cultural resistance. Thus, "Manzanar imagined himself as a kind of recycler. After all he, like other homeless in the city was a recycler of the last rung. The homeless were the insects and scavengers of society, feeding on leftovers, living in residue, collecting refuse, carting it this way and that for pennies. In the same manner, who would use the residue of sounds in the city if Manzanar did not?" (56). Manzanar's urban symphony, like Yamashita's literary olio of a novel, is a political and environmental response to consumer accumulation. Similarly, when the homeless take over the highway, what results is not entropic breakdown of order and productivity, but instead a fully functioning, alternative society; although lacking conventional social services like ambulances, the landscape is "surprisingly clean," with "regular trash pickup" and recycling (218–219). In *Tropic of Orange,* environmental sustainability is not the exclusive purview of liberal elites but the pragmatic mode of being of the underclasses—too often themselves treated as "trash"—for whom nothing is waste or wasted.

Yamashita's omnivorous literary imagination also embodies a commitment to interethnic coalition building. To Caroline Rody, *Tropic of Orange* "exemplifies the combined impact of the new transnational and interethnic paradigms on works of Asian American literature, becoming an allegory of imaginative 'paradigm shift' itself."[30] Similarly, Youngsuk Chae argues that "Yamashita indicates the necessity of forming an interethnic collaboration beyond rigid racial/ethnic boundaries and emphasizes that it is important for Asian Americans to react critically to the stereotypical image imposed upon them."[31] Such readings build on scholarly critiques of 1990s discourses of multiculturalism that too often celebrated racial difference in service of capitalism, like a United Colors of Benetton advertisement. Emi is a skeptic who pronounces that "cultural diversity is bullshit . . . It's a white guy in a Nirvana T-shirt and dreds" (128). Her point about multiculturalism as a form of cultural appropriation is underscored by a white woman at the sushi restaurant using chopsticks as hairpins and ignoring Emi's complex Asian American identity in favor of an idealized and static notion of "Japaneseness." Yet Yamashita slyly shows Emi to be similarly guilty of racial fetishization; Emi "had started dating Gabriel because he was Latino, part of that hot colorful race, only to find out that . . . he wasn't what you call the stereotype" (19). In this way, Yamashita shows that minorities often participate in the same kinds of multicultural objectification to which they are subjected by whites. Everyone is enmeshed in the circuits of capitalism that transform some citizens into valuable commodities and others into useless rubbish.

In this way, Yamashita demonstrates the dangers of what Jodi Melamed calls liberal multiculturalism's dual commitment to "represent" and "destroy" through a process of "misrecognition under which self-identified progressive whites could become active constituents for educational and municipal policies that exploited and abandoned impoverished communities of people of color."[32] The unnamed white restaurant patron surely votes against local policies that might support poor and minority people in her neighborhood. Similarly, Jeffrey Santa Ana sees *Tropic of Orange* as noteworthy for its pointed critique of Asian Americans' role in liberal multiculturalism: "To be Asian American in multicultural capitalist America means having to accommodate the perception that Asians not only represent a fetishized emotional product but also must perform it as agents of finance capital whose job, figuratively speaking, is to carry out the affective labor for the commodity happiness of liberal multiculturalism."[33] Emi and Gabriel benefit from their class privilege at the expense of other people of color. They sit sipping sake watching news accounts of firefighters who died in the highway disaster, comfortably distant from the danger and protected from poverty. Emi treats the news as entertainment, until she is mortally injured in the events she is filming. Similarly, only at the novel's end does Gabriel recognize his self-aggrandizing delusions about rescuing Rafaela and creating his own private utopia in Mexico as a result of his American wealth and privilege. Through Emi's overt criticisms of multiculturalism as a form of cultural tourism, as well as her and Bobby's fascination with material goods as a measure of success, Yamashita makes clear that Asian Americans are both victims of, and willing participants in, these exploitative processes.

The novel thus balances skepticism about multiculturalism with a sincere longing for interethnic community, most powerfully represented by the freeway reclamation. Sue-Im Lee describes this tension as Yamashita rejecting the false universalism inherent in the trope of the "global village," while yearning for forms of community that "can express the transnational, transcontinental nature of human existence without imperialist dimensions."[34] The novel's heroes are those like Buzzworm and the unnamed homeless creating new forms of community against the Darwinian struggle of the international marketplace. The encampment gestures toward the possibility of a multiracial alliance of the disenfranchised, who work together to create systems of value outside the logic of profit and loss. Whether Yamashita's celebration of small-scale solutions is a capitulation to the logic of neoliberalism or a prescient criticism of its dominant role in twenty-first-century public discourse is an open question.

CHAPTER 4

I Hotel

Karen Tei Yamashita's epic novel *I Hotel* (2010) explores history, memory, and Asian American community. *I Hotel* consists of ten interlinked novellas whose events occur between 1968 and 1977. The novel takes a broad look at Asian American political organizing and its connections to (and disjunctions from) other social movements in the period that were active in the San Francisco Bay Area and transnationally, such as the Third World Liberation Front, the American Indian movement, the Chicano movement, the civil rights and black power movements, the feminist movement, anti-war protests, and the movement for disability rights. But the work is also very much about Asian America's relationship to international movements and globalization. As Yamashita explained in an interview, "I wanted to figure out how the history fit—how the recuperation of Japanese American internment and Mao coming to power and the history of Korea, along with artistic practices, all fit. You know, there's something in 'Asian American' that is already diasporic, already transnational in these days. This thinking in this period predates the current interest in globalism, and I wanted to understand it."[1]

I Hotel demonstrates the promises and failures of coalition building throughout the 1960s and 1970s. As she did in *Tropic of Orange,* Yamashita here expresses skepticism toward identity politics and multiculturalism, while endorsing intercultural and transnational social activism. Similarly, Yamashita's critique of late-stage capitalism, so prominent in *Through the Arc of the Rain Forest* and *Tropic of Orange,* here focuses on an earlier moment in this process, when transnational connections led to collusion among multinational corporations, public agencies, and private institutions. These powerful transnational ties led to gentrification and overdevelopment.

Structure of the Book

I Hotel consists of ten novellas, each set in a different year (1968–1977), although events do not exclusively occur in that period. Each novella consists of multiple chapters featuring different characters and is told from different perspectives, using various genres. Yamashita gives voice to dozens of different characters' perspectives: Chinese Americans, Japanese Americans, Filipinos; members of the Black Panther Party, women's liberation activists, FBI spies; first-generation, second-generation, and third-generation Americans; young, old, and every age in-between. The novel's huge cast of characters debate, disagree with, and dismiss each other, while also falling in and out of love and struggling to create new forms of community. Yamashita recreates an era of profound idealism, when young people were passionately searching for political and social solutions without a common language or vision. She observed that the promise of the 1960s seemed to dissipate over time: "I think that the inability to resolve some of these questions, or to resolve them without the kind of passionate anger that people had—to the point of physically beating each other up—was part of the problem. It was partly because people were young and couldn't talk to each other, so those difficulties probably destroyed any kind of forward momentum."[2] Through the accretion of voices and concerns, it becomes increasingly difficult for the reader to synthesize the book into a singular, cohesive message. In this way, reading the book echoes Yamashita's sense of the era as a time of conflicting ideas.

The generic heterogeneity of the novel is similarly vertigo inducing. Yamashita writes in an astonishing array of forms: film scripts, standardized test questions, mock Confucian Analects, aphorisms in the style of Sun Tzu's *Art of War* and Mao's *Little Red Book*, news reporters' dispatches, transcriptions of a confidential FBI dossier, a memoir with folktale resembling Maxine Hong Kingston's *The Woman Warrior*, Native American mythology, a so-called "ethnic short story," poetry, a dance performance with music, and interview transcriptions. The novel also includes visual art such as illustrations and comics. The result is a dizzyingly complex portrait of a moment and a movement whose members periodically found common purpose together, but just as often splintered into competing efforts. No one person or character could see the whole. But there were a thousand points of entry and egress.

Yamashita's physical point of entry for this roiling period of American history is the International Hotel, a low-rent, single-room occupancy hotel on the corner of Kearny and Jackson streets in San Francisco. It was built in 1907, after the devastating 1906 earthquake and fire destroyed the previous building.

Throughout the 1920s and 1930s, the I Hotel housed thousands of migrant laborers who worked on farms and fisheries across the West Coast. Over time, the neighborhood became known as Manilatown due to the high proportion of Filipino migrants. Over the course of the next half century, the I Hotel became a site of political foment, cultural exchange, grassroots organizing, and artistic expression. During the 1960s and 1970s, the building housed many groups and individuals active in the yellow power movement and the Third World Liberation Front, as well as community organizations for Asian American cultural and artistic expression. In Yamashita's novel, the I Hotel serves as both the symbolic and literal home of the Asian American community.

Much as Yamashita opens *Tropic of Orange* with a set of "HyperContexts" as a way of tracking the movements of characters through time and space, *I Hotel* begins with a set of ten diagrams, each one a two-dimensional representation of a three-dimensional cube corresponding to one novella. These diagrams serve as précis summarizing each novella's critical year, major historical event, key characters, and a theme and/or artistic form being explored; they are shorthand for the who/what/when/where/how of each novella. These diagrams also function to raise questions about how we construct meaning about the past, and what is lost when one translates experience into narrative. By visualizing history as three-dimensional "stories" (in both senses of the word—as narratives and as layers of a building) of the I Hotel, and then unfolding those stories into a two-dimensional diagram, Yamashita asks her readers to consider what is lost in that flattening. How does the process of trying to tell history shift or distort the meaning of those events and relationships? And, intriguingly, what topics become literally adjacent as we "build" up these stories vertically?

Yamashita credits *I Hotel*'s genesis to influential Asian American studies professor Amy Ling at the University of Wisconsin–Madison, who invited Yamashita to contribute to an edited volume in the 1990s.[3] Yamashita wrote a satirical scholarly article complete with invented footnotes; titled "Siamese Twins and Mongoloids: Cultural Appropriation and the Deconstruction of Stereotype Via the Absurdity of Humor," the essay critiqued an imagined novel written by "Karen Tei Yamashita."[4] Yamashita's project for Ling explored how the Asian American and black power movements "have been eaten up by the academy in the sense that ethnic studies programs created in this period [the late 1960s and 1970s] now have to produce the same kind of work that they were perhaps rebelling against."[5] After writing her work of faux criticism, Yamashita decided to actually write the novel she was imagining about the 1960s and 1970s.[6] The project quickly centered on the Third World Liberation Front strikes at San Francisco State College and the University of California, Berkeley, and ultimately, the community organizing efforts to save the International Hotel in downtown San Francisco. Yamashita again found herself deep in historical research. Echoing her process for *Brazil-Maru, I Hotel* was the culmination of ten years of archival research and writing, including interviewing and listening to oral histories of 140 people. Yamashita was both a witness and an outsider to the events that occur in *I Hotel*: "I was on the younger end watching what was happening. I graduated high school in 1969 and had some kind of relationship to it through high school in Gardena, in Los Angeles. [Gardena High School] was Japanese American—maybe 50–60% Japanese American, sansei children of nisei who come out of the camps. So there was an investment in this new vision" of Asian America.[7] The novel provides readers this sense of being both inside and outside various social movements of the period, in the process providing a kaleidoscopic view that no single person could ever have. She credits Allan Kornblum, the editor and publisher of Coffee House Press, with deciding that it was all part of one epic book, rather than a series of ten small books.[8]

Compared to her previous work, *I Hotel's* cast of characters is exponentially larger. Rone Shavers described the novel as "an encyclopedic text" and Yamashita's process as "reconstructing history" because she blurs the line between fact and fiction, quotation and invention, imagined and historical figures.[9] The novel features real-life figures of the era, such as San Francisco State College interim president S. I. Hayakawa and Asian American novelists Maxine Hong Kingston and Frank Chin, as well as composites of real-life figures. For example, "Mo Akagi" has elements of activists Mo Nishida and Richard Aoki, while "Edmund Yat Min Lee" resembles Ling-chi Wang, who taught ethnic studies at UC Berkeley. "Arthur Hama" shares biographical elements with Takeo "Edward" Terada, a Japanese immigrant who painted some of the Coit Tower murals, while "Arthur Ma" is a version of Victor Wong, a beatnik artist and journalist featured in Jack Kerouac's last book *Big Sur.* Other characters appear to have been invented from whole cloth, while still being representative of people and patterns of the era. For example, in the 1975 novella, Yamashita's fictional Harry Hama is a participant in real historical events when, on April 5, 1977, he is one of "sixty handicapped persons [who] take over the fourth floor of the San Francisco regional offices of the United States Department of Health, Education, and Welfare" (521). Those disability right activists camped out for almost a month, growing to more than a hundred people who refused to leave until President Jimmy Carter's administration agreed to implement a 1973 law protecting the rights of people with disabilities.

The novel continually questions the best medium and method for capturing and dramatizing history, be it painting, poetry, performance, film, fiction, or oral history. Moreover, Yamashita shows how even the same ostensible medium creates very different atmospheres and messages depending on the artist and their particular approach (for example social realism vs. abstraction). In its multivocal form, the novel refuses any definitive answer, instead creating a mosaic of voices, stories, and genres that correspond to the plethora of social issues and activist methods of the era. Yamashita gives voice to the suspicion some activists have toward non-realist modes of representation; the character Estelle Hama, an avowed communist and social realist artist, rejects fiction as a form because it "twists the truth. It's all lies" (513). And yet, Yamashita shows how Estelle fictionalizes what happened to her husband Arthur; she tells her two sons that Art died, while in fact he left and married another woman in Japan. In this way, the novel highlights the contradictions between art and life, politics and representation, memory and history. Politics and art are made by human beings whose frailties shape their approaches. Just as there is no one "right" path to social change, there is no single best mode of expression.

The novel also demonstrates the various forms of affiliation and adjacency among the social movements of the era by showing how characters in one novella (or "story") show up in other plots, connected by personal histories and shared politics. For example, Olivia Wang (from the 1972 novella) sends Stony Ima to Alcatraz to support the American Indian protests there (1973); one of the Alcatraz activists, Ria Ishii, previously dated Mo Akagi (1970) and James Baba (1969); Wayne Takabayashi (1973) is the son of Tom Takabayashi, who was a criminology professor at Berkeley during the Third World Liberation Front strikes (1969). Art and Estelle Hama (1975) once lived in the Monkey Building, where Paul Lin's dad lived (1968). Sen Hama's (1975) roommate is James Baba (1969) and Sen creates images of Goro, a.k.a. Nelson Lopez, an activist on the run after being accused of killing a police officer (1969; 1971). Tom (1969) shows up at the exhibition of Estelle's drawings and letters from her time in internment (1975). Virgilio, Devin, and Abra Balcena appear in multiple novellas (1974, 1976). This intratextuality emphasizes the dense web of connections among activists, artists, and radicals of the era.

Yamashita also emphasizes the historical and familial echoes that resound through time and across ethnic lines. As these various stories accumulate, the reader recognizes that parallels function as a kind of internal rhyme, such as the similarities between Arthur Hama (1975) and Arthur Ma (1976), two Asian American artists in interracial relationships who had children they abandoned. Yet for their obvious similarities, there are also key differences, as Arthur Ma did not know he had a child until Egan showed up decades later, while Arthur Hama willfully left one wife and family behind to start another family in Japan. These echoes serve as reminders of the way that history is not inevitable, but is in fact made of a million individual decisions, of other paths not taken.

The I Hotel building becomes a protagonist in the story, with its own spirit and energy. As Michael Zisler described in his review, "The symbolic significance of the hotel is clear: it serves as the crucible in which the many varied traditions of Asian immigrants were temporarily united in defense of the poorest among them."[10] Over time, the I Hotel served the entire Asian American community in a multitude of ways, for a multitude of purposes, including a pool hall, a community center, the Chinatown Youth Service Center, the hungry i nightclub, a silkscreen print shop, a sweatshop, and a cooperative sewing shop. Yet the value of the I Hotel is not merely in its building, but in the web of relations made possible. As one of the longtime residents notes sadly, "Saving the building is not the same thing as saving the hotel. Maybe anyone can save the building. Harder to save the hotel" (446). Yamashita's novel is an effort to save the hotel by memorializing the ideas and affiliations that the hotel sparked.

Simultaneously, Yamashita explores how geography constructs race, and how race shapes place, through a legal landscape that continually restricted Asian American property ownership. Through the stories of various characters, readers learn about the history of Chinatowns (and other minority enclaves), which were effectively ghettos to which Asian immigrants and their heirs were relegated, due to laws throughout the nineteenth and early twentieth centuries that prevented Asian Americans from purchasing property in other neighborhoods. Decades later, during World War II, Japanese Americans had their homes, businesses, and property confiscated while they were themselves imprisoned in internment camps. These histories of Asian American displacement are put in dialogue with other groups' histories of forced migration and relocation, such as Indian removal and the prison island of Alcatraz. The novel emphasizes the common experiences among different minority groups in the United States, without losing sight of specific contexts and conditions. Yamashita connects these histories of displacement to neoliberal global economics that prioritize white-owned investment capital far more than they do the local people of color who call those places home. Through reference to these many prehistories and related histories of the fight for the future of the International Hotel, the novel illustrates the variety of ways that U.S. citizenship has not guaranteed the free exercise of human, civil, or legal rights. Such history also serves to make evident that the supposed "failure to assimilate" of Asian Americans (and other minority groups)—which was the object of white culture's criticisms—was actually the direct result of state policies.

Historical Context for *I Hotel*

As with the characters, events in the novel are a combination of the meticulously documented and the wholly imagined. Yamashita alludes to and invents a multitude of events of the period that involved Asian Americans either centrally or peripherally, such as the arrest of Wendy Yoshimura for her participation in the activities of the Symbionese Liberation Army, the occupation of Alcatraz by Native American activists from 1969 through 1971, and the murder of Evelyn Okubo and the attempted murder of Ranko Carol Yamada in Chicago in 1970, presumably perpetrated by the Black Panthers. These historical footnotes create a rich context for Yamashita's exploration of the fissures and fusions among various minority coalitions, as well as between individual activists.

In 1968 the Third World Liberation Front (TWLF), a coalition of various student groups—including the Black Student Union (BSU), the Latin American Student Organization (LASO), the Mexican American Student Confederation (MASC), the Philippine American Collegiate Endeavor (PACE), the Native American Students Union, and Intercollegiate Chinese for Social Action (ICSA)—came together at San Fransisco State College to fight for a more diverse, representative, and socially engaged college curriculum and to protest the Vietnam War. In November 1968, students at SFSC (now San Francisco State University) went on strike. In January 1969, students at the University of California, Berkeley did the same. Influenced by the Black Panthers and the Chicano/a movement, the TWLF demanded that colleges and universities redress the erasure of Asian American, Black, Chicano, and Native histories in their curriculum. After months of protests and increasing police repression, in March 1969 the TWLF won two major victories: UC Berkeley agreed to create the first ethnic studies department in the United States, and San Francisco State developed the nation's first College of Ethnic Studies, inspiring the development of ethnic studies curricula across the nation. As Harvey Dong explains, "Not only was the study of American history revolutionized, the struggle for ethnic studies became part of a revolutionary movement."[11] This moment is often considered the beginning of the Asian American movement as well because various Asian American groups participated in the TWLF organizing, and pan-Asian identification and activism developed.

Moreover, some of the greatest violence of the civil rights, black power, and anti-Vietnam War protests occurred in 1968. Martin Luther King, Jr. was assassinated in April of that year, sparking rioting in many cities, including Baltimore, Chicago, Kansas City, Louisville, and Washington, D.C. Robert Kennedy was murdered that June. The launch of the Tet Offensive in January of 1968 marked a turning point against support for the Vietnam War, as it became obvious the war was unwinnable. On the cultural front, Woodstock marked the apex of the free-love era in August 1968, while murder and mayhem at Altamont in December closed out the year with senseless violence. The

Democratic National Convention protests further eroded young people's confidence in official politics and state institutions.

In this period, gentrification in San Francisco increasingly encroached on Manilatown and other minority neighborhoods. In 1968, the I Hotel was deemed a blighted property and targeted for redevelopment as a parking garage. In 1977, after a decade of community protests, the residents of the hotel, mostly poor and elderly Asian men living on social security, were forcibly evicted by police; the hotel was finally demolished in 1981. Making matters worse, the site remained derelict for more than a decade after financing fell through for the proposed development. Finally, after ongoing community activism, the International Hotel Manilatown Center opened in 2005 to provide senior housing and a community center. Almost a dozen of the new residents had been occupants of the original I Hotel.

The hotel remains a potent symbol of the problems of gentrification, particularly for low-income, immigrant, and minority residents. As the *Oakland Post* reported at the time, "For years community organizations have fought 'red-lining' practices by banks and insurance companies that effectively denied credit to certain neighborhoods. Ironically, the activists' successes, combined with an upturn in the real estate market, often meant that lenders have become more willing to make loans in older neighborhoods. But the loans have been going to different people—wealthy individuals buying up the older housing stock for conversion to townhouses and expensive condominiums."[12] While San Francisco city officials seek to avoid a repeat of the public relations disaster that was the demolition of the I Hotel, the problems of housing rights, development, and affordability have only gotten worse; San Francisco is now the most expensive city in the nation due to the economic boom caused by the technology industry.

The Novel

The first novella, "1968: Eye Hotel," opens with Chinese American student Paul Lin learning about his father's death at Lunar New Year. Told primarily through third-person narration, analects, and film scripts, we learn about Paul's activities in the Third World Liberation Front strikes at San Francisco State College, where he is a student in Chen Wen-guang's Chinese literature class. His classmate is Edmund Yat Lee, a hardworking student who must put himself through school. Edmund perceives activism to be a luxury for middle-class kids who don't need to work, although he is eventually persuaded to get involved (15). Tragically, Edmund dies after being shot at a garment factory strike. Chen is a closeted gay man who, Paul later learns, was briefly married to Paul's mother. This novella dramatizes the second generation's estrangement from both ethnic cultural customs and their own parents. Paul knows nothing about the rules for a Chinese funeral; his aunt makes all the preparations. Despite his father's atheism and existentialism, as his aunt opines, "All that's irrelevant when you die in Chinatown" (5). But Paul also comes to realize how little he knew about his parents, including his father's previous life as an artist or his mother's first marriage. The political turns out to be deeply personal for Paul. However, in contrast to most 1960s narratives positing the intractable "generation gap" between baby boomers and their parents, Paul's activism actually brings him closer to his father, even after his father's death.

In "1969: I Spy Hotel," echoes of Japanese internment during World War II reverberate with COINTELPRO spying on activists in the 1960s. In both periods, racial minorities in the United States were treated as dangerous, traitorous, and disposable in the face of paranoia about international enemies, particularly those in Asia. And yet, Yamashita shows that Asian American student activists, inspired by black power, demonstrated increasing commitment to the local community, as when UC Berkeley student activists add the I Hotel as a "community field component" to Professor Tom Takabayashi's Asian American Experience course. At the same time as these activists are being monitored by the U.S. government as "subversives," they are fighting the forces of privatization within the Japanese American business class, whose goals are furthered by the Nihonmachi Community Development Corporation, which is attempting to negotiate with the city to create and control a tourist-friendly Japantown to serve business interests, rather than community residents. The forces of government and commerce align against community interests.

In "1970: 'I' Hotel," Yamashita further explores Afro-Asian connections in the Asian American and black power movements. Mo Akagi (modeled in part on Richard Aoki) is a Japanese American active in the Black Panthers who is in Moscow in 1970 to talk about Communism along with members of the Red Guard Party. With chapter titles like "I Am a Brother," "I Am a Martial Artist," "I Am the Third World," and "I Am a Revolutionary," Yamashita emphasizes the affinities and influences between social protest movements that sought to fight both American racism and U.S. imperialism. The empowerment of this interracial coalition is undercut by the sexism of the era, with women doing much of the unsung work of the movement. In this story Yamashita refuses either to simply celebrate the "good old days" or to dismiss the era for its failures. Rather she emphasizes the complexities of social movements, and the particular difficulties women of color have faced in order to be heard.

"1971: Aiiieeeee! Hotel" centers on the mythology of outlaws in Asian American storytelling and history. This novella explores different ways that Asian American "outlaws" have rejected conventional masculinity and femininity. Blending realism and fantasy, Sandy Hu is a Chinese American poet, actress, and singer who is also an outlaw swordswoman. She teams up with Lady Murasaki, a figure from Japanese literature reimagined as an Asian American Foxy Brown; together they reenact various Asian American female "types" in American popular culture. This novella similarly transforms Chinese American literary titans Maxine Hong Kingston and Frank Chin into folk heroes, rendered in comic book format: Son and Daughter, Chinaman and Chinawoman, Patriarch and Matriarch. We also get an exploration of doubles and doppelgängers, with Chinese American outlaw and jazz saxophonist Gerald K. Li meeting a second Gerald Li, a white man with a Chinese name who plays saxophone "with an Oriental chinkified sound," and a third Gerald K. Li who is a fan from Stockton. At a gig set up by the Stockton Gerald, the first Gerald meets his physical doppelgänger, the bartender Joe Sung; Joe believes Gerald is his brother, the poet Jack Sung. This novella uses genre tropes to illustrate the ways that all Asians are presumed by whites to look alike, as well as how white cultural appropriation is often more commercially successful than minority artistic originality.

In "1972: Inter-national Hotel," readers experience a revolutionary romance between Olivia Wang, a Chinese American daughter of privilege, and Ben San Pablo, the working-class grandson of a manong, a Filipino man who migrated to the United States to work as an agricultural or other low-wage laborer. Ben is all revolutionary theory while Olivia represents praxis, including volunteering for the Student Nonviolent Coordinating Committee in Mississippi. They debate, fall in love, and have a baby named Malcolm (after Malcolm X). Echoing infamous conflicts in the civil rights, black power, and student movements, Yamashita shows how women are too often treated as secretaries, cooks, wives, or prostitutes in service to male leadership. Ben and Olivia's relationship embodies this gendered division of labor in the revolution, with Olivia treated as merely the "practitioner of his theorizing" (301). But then she gets ovarian cancer and dies, and it is her materiality that he misses with his whole body and mind. This story has all the pathos of an Asian American version of *Love Story*, while looking with a gimlet eye at the ways that life, in all its messy beauty, has a way of complicating and tempering youthful idealism and abstract theorizing.

"1973: Int'l Hotel" uses creation myths to show the power of interethnic coalitions. The histories of Asian Americans and American Indians are intertwined on Alcatraz Island, as three Asian American activists—Stony Ima, Ria Ishii, and Wayne Takabayashi—bring supplies to the American Indian activists occupying the former prison island. Yamashita emphasizes the connections between the Indian reservation, the Japanese internment camp, and the prison, while demonstrating the power of interethnic coalitions to transcend these barriers: "The feeling of excitement and purpose was palpable everywhere. How many times in your life do you feel that kind of power, the sort that unifies a people in collective pride and knowing? . . . A connective wave carries you to the same infinite space, and you feel more alive than you have ever felt" (380). Back at the I Hotel, Ria Ishii and Mrs. Lee create a cooperative sewing shop where Chinese women immigrants create Mao jackets to be sold as trendy fashion items (385). Radical politics and commerce mix, often uneasily. Characters experience mystical visions that may or may not be (merely) acid trips. The promise of the multiethnic coalition seems lost when the government takes back Alcatraz from the activists and designates it a national park (399). The effort to memorialize the history of the place comes at the expense of people of color, whose ties to the land are once again erased.

"1974: I-Migrant Hotel" focuses on food as a means of cultural transmission and community building. Felix Allos is a Filipino manong who claims to have cooked for Cesar Chavez and made hooch for John Steinbeck; he has lived in the I Hotel for fifty years, and is now facing eviction. The loss of the I Hotel is the loss of the only home he has known. Through his cooking, Felix communicates his feelings of love, desire, loss, nostalgia, and homesickness. Abra Balcena is a single mother and lesbian feminist activist who also lives in the I Hotel, and for whom Felix has unrequited feelings. Abra's father hung around with Carlos Bulosan and wrote for Communist papers (459). Macario Amado is a student activist collecting oral histories of the old-timers in the I Hotel. Through hunger and plenty, the residents of the I Hotel bond over shared food, memories, and hopes. But this community is now being removed, as the novella ends with protesters at the hotel being beaten by police. Memories are all that will be left.

"1975: Internationale Hotel" centers on the Hama family—Arthur, Estelle, and their sons Sen and Harry—two generations of activists who argue about the role of art in the revolution. Arthur was a Communist, an anti-fascist, an activist and a muralist who went to jail for being a suspected spy for Japan. Art eventually joined the U.S. military intelligence and fought in Burma before becoming a peace activist. He left the United States for Japan in 1951 because of McCarthy-era red-baiting (502). Unbeknownst to his children, there he fell in love with another woman, so he stayed until his death in 1974. Estelle is a white artist who comes to understand anti-Japanese racism through her relationship with Art. She goes with Arthur to the Tule Lake internment camp during World War II, and there is almost shot while holding an infant Sen. She documents her outrage by painting hundreds of watercolors. Sen is an artist, drawing comics and making silkscreens for various political causes. His younger brother Harry is an activist in the TWLF protests and leader of the early disability rights movement. Despite his participation in the 1968 TWLF protests and 1976 disability rights protests, Harry literally cannot get arrested as a man in a wheelchair, but he does meet Clara, a fellow activist with whom he falls in love (525). Years later, after continued advocacy for public access for people with disabilities, Harry is arrested, finally getting his wish to be taken seriously. Estelle's children come to understand her better when her art and letters from internment are displayed at Japantown Art and Media. "This is not an exhibition," she complains. Her son Sen concurs, "No, it's a story finally revealed" (505). Like *I Hotel* the novel, Estelle's art exhibition blends art and history to recreate the emotional lives of a particular time and place. There is no "pure" mode of representation, for each of the family members chooses different mediums of expression and political causes. The debates among the Hama family suggest the internal disagreements within all social movements, and the forms of love that bind them together. These political successes and familial bonds are tempered by the tragic death of Sen, who dies in a motorcycle accident at Tule Lake, the site of the family's incarceration. Love and loss are universal experiences.

The next novella, "1976: Ai Hotel," features seven doomed romantic couples who meet and rendezvous at the I Hotel. With repeated allusions to the myth of Orpheus and Eurydice and similar versions of this tragic romance plot in Asian art and literature, these stories highlight love's hold even after death. Art and poetry become the means of keeping love (and the memory of sex) alive through the ravages of time and separation. Devin and Yuri are young people who live in the I Hotel. He is a poet who is in love with her, but she is in love with someone else. When she dies of an overdose, Devin loses his mind and is institutionalized. Once he is well, he returns to the hotel to interview manongs for an oral history project. After a while, the manongs start recording their own stories. Virgilio is one of those old-timers who recalls his own doomed love affair with Momo, whom he met while picking fruit for her father in the Central Valley when he was young; Virgilio got Momo pregnant, and she hanged herself. He is haunted by her memory. Sophie is a nude model for Arthur Ma, a former art professor who has a studio in the basement of the hotel; her beloved is Egan, a poet and Arthur's son from a relationship with a black woman. Sophie and Egan share a love for Chinese erotica. Sophie gets pregnant, but when Egan is killed in action in Vietnam, Sophie puts their baby up for adoption and moves to Tokyo. Stony and Aiko fall in love through letters while the former is in prison, bonding over dreams of revolution; their first meeting after he is paroled is a consummation of erotics and politics. Clio and Abra are active in the women's movement; they are "poetry sisters" trying to find love and their literary voices. Bard and Huo Lian fall in love while doing a Chikamatsu play together, blending into their appointed roles as tragic lovers, even though Bard is engaged to someone else. Yuri's sister Renee, after going through a divorce and grieving Yuri's death, is now in a relationship with Ken, the founder of the Asian Law Caucus; after two miscarriages, she fears sex for the heartbreak it might bring. Taken together, this novella explores the losses that love can survive, as well as those that love and sex cannot heal. Politics are subsumed in the small and large tragedies of human existence.

The final novella, "1977: I-Hotel," recounts the final chapter of the hotel's life, when the protestors are unable to save the hotel and its residents are forcibly removed. This novella fully personifies the hotel, with its "death" turned into a public spectacle being recorded for posterity on audio and video: "And that was when the life of the I Hotel was finally snuffed out—our hearing gone deaf, our seeing windows blinded, our fierce voices silenced" (587). Yet this last novella also reminds readers that, just as the I Hotel had at least three lives in three different buildings, the spirit of the place will live on in new sites even after this building is demolished. The three characters at the center are Judy Eng, capturing video; Mr. Chang, broadcasting audio; and the collective "we" of the hotel and its defenders witnessing these events.[13] Yamashita highlights how audio and video together document history but require an audience to understand and give meaning to those events. The I Hotel was a refuge for thousands of people for whom it offered an alternative vision of "home" and "nation" (590), providing a haven for Asian American subjects not welcomed into, included in, or assimilated into white, heteronormative American middle-class life (590). The book *I Hotel* serves as an attempt to re-member (as in put back together for the purposes of reanimation) this haunted, haunting place. Here Yamashita's melancholic take on history and memory is fully on display. The book stands as a monument to a heterogeneous site that meant different things to many people. It was a site for community formation and communion, as well as disagreement and division. And so, the last words of the book remind readers of this complicated legacy: "And in time we may remember, collecting every little memory, all the bits and pieces, into a larger memory, rebuilding a great layered and labyrinthine, now imagined, international hotel of many rooms, the urban experiment of a homeless community built to house the needs of temporary lives. And for what? To resist death and dementia. To haunt a disappearing landscape. To forever embed this geography with our visions and voices. To kiss the past and you good-bye, leaving the indelible spit of our DNA on still moist lips. Sweet. Sour. Salty. Bitter" (605). Yamashita thus reminds readers that history is not something to be "preserved," but something that must be actively created by a collective.

Reviews and Scholarship: *I Hotel*

As David Palumbo-Liu makes clear, "as much as it is historically accurate and broadly revelatory of new and old histories, *I Hotel* is a work of fiction. It conveys, with nuance and often irony, the human motivations—good, bad, honorable, egotistical, wise, naïve—behind the story."[14] The National Book Award committee, which named *I Hotel* a finalist for its prestigious award, praised the work precisely for the boldness and originality of its treatment of historical events: "stylistically innovative, vertiginous, and sweeping, the novel achieves a miraculous blend of fact and fiction."[15]

Not all readers found the novel's ambitions effective. Writing for *SF Gate,* Vanessa Hua felt the book "sacrifices sustained narrative momentum in the interest of telling a broad range of stories. Some readers may wish Yamashita had gone deeper into the lives so tantalizingly glimpsed."[16] More damningly, in the *Chicago Tribune* Alan Cheuse wrote that *I Hotel* "stands as the single most ambitious and experimental work of fiction I have read in a long, long time. But her yearning to put into a single volume all of the striving, confusion, successes and failures of an entire generation of Asian-Americans living in San Francisco in the 1970s doesn't seem to have done more than made for a glorious failure of a book."[17] Such criticisms refuse to take the novel on its own terms, desiring instead a more conventional take on the era of which Yamashita writes. Readers who embrace Yamashita's experimentalism are rewarded with a complex portrait of a particular time and place that goes well beyond familiar portraits or platitudes.

Over the course of its six hundred pages, the novel consistently explores the 1960s maxim that the personal is political. Yamashita explained, "What I wanted to say is that all of these things were personal to people, that they felt it in their skin. They knew these things had happened to themselves and their families—it was personal for them when they started—but then it became something much larger than themselves."[18] In *I Hotel,* Yamashita gets inside the skins of dozens of characters, imagining the personal convictions and familial dramas that shaped the political era in incalculable ways.

Various scholars have analyzed particular novellas' modeling of politics through personal relationships. Nathan Ragain focuses on the couple as a model for the tensions in the personal-is-political mantra of the era, as embodied in the 1972 novella: "Yamashita reimagines the romantic couple as a figure for the complex dialectic between personal identity and prolonged struggle and between particularity and universality. That is, . . . the forms of both the novel and the romantic couple open onto a universalist politics without erasing the conflicts that arise from their particular positions."[19] Chris Eng emphasizes the potential to rethink intergenerational relationships—in literature as in activism—and to consider how queer desire might operate in those contexts; he analyzes the characters of Paul Wallace Lin and his mentor Chen Wen-guang in the 1968 novella, explaining how "*I Hotel* transfigures the meaning of generation as a noun referring to a discrete unit partitioned by temporal boundaries to a constellation of longings and actions by which we cohere to generate movements."[20] *I Hotel,* with its capacious approach, encourages a variety of discrete readings to unpack the various forms of affiliation it models.

Formally, one of the distinguishing features of *I Hotel* is its assumed Asian American audience. Or rather, the novel immerses the reader deep within the Asian American movement, rather than first defining terms and introducing key figures' significance to a presumed white audience. In this way, the novel demands its readers do the work of recognizing the touchstones of Asian American history, literature, and politics. For students unfamiliar with Angel Island, paper sons and picture brides, bachelor communities, Japanese internment, the republication of Asian American authors like John Okada, or the literary battle between Maxine Hong Kingston and Frank Chin, reading *I Hotel* can feel confusing, alienating, and overwhelming. In effect, Yamashita inverts the experience of minority subjects in the United States who are expected to know mainstream (read: white, elite, male) U.S. history, literature, and culture. By contrast, Yamashita's approach has the revolutionary effect of truly centering Asian American experience—something almost unheard of in mainstream histories of the 1960s and 1970s.

At the level of language, Yamashita humorously explores various familiar metaphors for Asian American experience. For example, she describes the hyphenated identity of "Asian-American" as akin to being "half this–half that" as if caught between "schizophrenia and assimilation" (231). White Americans presume a perpetual divide between an ethnic past and an American present. Similarly, in a comic book sequence featuring "Anna Mae Wong and Suzie Wong" as the conjoined twins of Chiquita Banana, she explores the stereotypes of being "yellow on the outside, white on the inside," with one sister fitting the model minority stereotype and the other the bad girl (262). Chiquita's sister is Mulan Rouge (pun very much intended), who avenges Chiquita's death by separating the twins. What does it mean that a formerly conjoined pair are now separate racial stereotypes? The novel complicates such binary thinking by portraying a huge spectrum of Asian American experiences that make such cartoon portrayals seem all the more ridiculous.

In a similar way, Yamashita explores familial metaphors to depict the roles of Asian American ethnic groups to each other, and to the United States. In the 1971 novella, Maxine Hong Kingston and Frank Chin are alternately depicted in illustrations by Sina Grace as son and daughter, sister and brother, Ba and Ma (father and mother), and patriarch and matriarch of Asian American literature, among other roles. Asian Americans are repeatedly described as "orphans" in America. Later in that same novella, Yamashita gives us this gem, credited to Pearl Buck: "Once a man is orphaned, he is free to create himself, to be self-made. Orphaned brothers are free to reformulate their loyalties, wresting brotherly power and territory from emperors, usurpers, usurers, priests, and bureaucrats" (237). The orphan is cut off from his or her familial past, left to an uncertain future without the comforting guidance of a parent. Yamashita shows this to be an apt metaphor for the first generation of "Asian Americans" struggling to define themselves and their place in the United States and to create new models of affiliation.[21]

Yamashita connects this idea of the orphan to that of the doppelgänger, or double. This metaphor interrogates American stereotypes that imagine Asian subjects as either "model minorities" or the "yellow peril." Yamashita uses the double in yet another way, in order to explore the psychological consequences of popular culture that turns complex ethnic cultures into kitsch. A few chapters later in the 1971 novella, the narrator asks, "Honey, you might be an orphaned brother, but what happens when you meet your orphaned double? In the case of the doppelganger, who is who? Who is real and who is fake?" (265). The predominance of ethnic stereotypes, and the absence of diverse representations of Asian Americans, makes it hard to know what is actually "true." As Lai Ying Yu indicates, the Asian American movement asked, "Was there a single and ineffable identity that could be defined as Asian American? And if so, what was it?"[22] In *I Hotel,* Yamashita restlessly explores this search for distinctive cultural forms that reflect Asian American experience. Sandy Hu asks, "But what is Asian American dance? . . . What's the memory of the Asian American body?" (279). The Asian American movement thus sought to develop new identities, models of affiliation, and aesthetic forms.

In terms of the novel's relationship to existing generic categories, A. Robert Lee describes the novel as an extraordinary exploration of "fiction-as-memory." He continues, "The hotel, in Yamashita's compendious but carefully deliberate architectonics serves as Asian America's gathering reflection, room for room stories, basement to rooftop metaphors of each contributing and cross-plied ethnicity . . . The effect is a massive work of memorialization, a crosshatch of storytelling, at once taken up with Asian California lives and collectives yet full of even more inclusive period excavation and popular culture."[23] The novel's fictionalization serves to emphasize this historical archive and to model it spatially.

Other scholars have emphasized the connections between *I Hotel* and Yamashita's earlier works. Wen Jin considers *I Hotel* to be an extension and culmination of Yamashita's earlier "fantastical fiction," arguing that "The novel does not depict just one Asian American movement, but two different conceptions of the movement that cannot be easily ranked. These two conceptions are embodied in the two different configurations of the fantastical in the novel, one spectacular and formative, the other inconspicuous and transformative. The former can be correlated with the idea of a grand social movement that calls into being a pan-ethnic community, while the latter is correlated with the vision of a still emerging, shifting social formation grounded in shared struggles over memory and identity."[24]

The novel's careful attention to the particularities of Asian American experience directly leads to its exploration of an array of interethnic alliances, rivalries, and tensions to which the 1960s gave birth. Yamashita gives voice to the deep kinship of Afro-Asian relations through the Black power and Yellow power movements and shows how governmental institutions like the police and FBI sought to undermine these minority alliances. Moments of possibility are accompanied by disagreements that threaten hard-won unity. The coalitional politics that lead to change in the Third World Liberation Front protests that open the novella are fragile, as participants have as many differences as they do common interests. Yamashita illustrates disagreements about tactics, debates about whether to prioritize ethnically specific concerns or pan-ethnic issues, conflicts over different experiences separating ethnic groups of the same race, and generational divides between American-born children and immigrant parents or grandparents, giving new significance to debates about the "generation gap" of the 1960s student movements.

Another major theme of the novel is Yamashita's consideration of transnational and diasporic connections as alternatives to capitalist social relations. Lily Wong considers the ways in which Yamashita "dwells" over China in *I Hotel,* by which she means both obsessing about the past and occupying physical space in order to imagine new forms of diasporic consciousness: "Drawing from 'Chinese connections' to revitalize a pivotal time in U.S. movement politics, Yamashita creates minor transnational attachments: she decenters ideas of the nation-state (be it the United States or China) and ruptures narratives of global capital accumulation in a neoliberal order."[25]

While Yamashita's novel is rightly credited with bringing the past vividly to life, *I Hotel* is also noteworthy for its unsentimental reflection on representations of the era. Yamashita rejects the nostalgia that typically accompanies works about the 1960s. As Olivia says, "Knowing the story's end does not necessarily imply completion or knowledge, for if many endings are possible, so also are many beginnings. History may proceed sequentially or, as they say, *must* proceed sequentially, but stories may turn and turn again—the knowing end kissing the innocent beginning, the innocent end kissing the knowing beginning" (Yamashita 301). Through moments like this and the whole Tower of Babel structure of the tome, Yamashita reminds readers that although we behave as though history proceeds inevitably and causally, there is nothing fated about it. History is a series of opportunities taken as well as those missed, of happenstance and luck, of retrospective and prospective interpretations of events. The 1960s and 1970s was a time of profound alliance making among interconnected people and movements, but there was nothing inevitable about what happened. Yamashita shows how related were various social movements, how enmeshed with questions of power and justice, representation and change; and yet she refuses at every turn to give readers easy, familiar narratives of the 1960s and 1970s. There is no single moment when the promise of the era collapsed into discord. In fact, there was no halcyon moment when absolutely anything was possible. The past does not fail us; rather, we continually fail to recognize the myriad challenges that make social change so hard to enact and so difficult to maintain.

CHAPTER 5

Anime Wong

Some of Yamashita's theatrical and performance works, far less well known than her efforts in other genres, were published in *Anime Wong: Fictions of Performance* (2014), edited by Stephen Hong Sohn. Yamashita's theatrical works not included in that collection are quite difficult to access, and none of her performance works had long theatrical lives.[1] Though Yamashita's theatrical and performance works were even more ephemeral than theater usually is—most of her produced work was given only two- or three-day runs—the period in which Yamashita wrote these works was crucial for her development as an artist. Throughout the 1980s and 1990s Yamashita experimented with theater, musicals, multimedia, and performance art. She refined her use of point of view as a result of hearing her words spoken aloud on stage. As she described, "I learned in this process to listen to or to hear the voices of my characters, that narrative voice is a construction that is open to interpretation but requires a cadence and syntax. Hearing actors recite what I wrote made me think about what I heard and what they were hearing."[2] More than two decades later, she returned to writing performances for the edited volume, adding several new pieces that extend and expand her ideas about Asian Americans in popular culture.

Anime Wong collects six of Yamashita's theatrical pieces from the 1980s to 1990s, plus three newer works, along with photographs, playbills, publicity material, musical scores, and other ephemera into a kind of performance scrapbook. The volume is not meant to be a comprehensive record of Yamashita's theatrical career. Rather, Sohn and Yamashita worked together to craft a coherent volume organized around key themes. Most of the works are united by a concern for economic relations between the United States and Asia, along with satirical reworkings of the science fiction trope of "techno-Orientalism," coined by David Morley and Kevin Robins.[3] Made famous by quintessential 1980s sci-fi works like Ridley Scott's film *Blade Runner* (1982) and William Gibson's book *Neuromancer* (1984), techno-Orientalism is the idea, as Yamashita noted, that Asian Americans are "implicated in the future as global citizens and transnational subjects."[4] Sohn and Yamashita omitted texts that were unfinished, incomplete, or thematically unrelated.[5] The three new works—*Anime Wong: A CyberAsian Odyssey* (2008), *Siamese Twins and Mongoloids* (2012), and *Jan Ken Pon* (2012)—were written contemporaneously with, or specifically for, the volume *Anime Wong: Fictions of Performance.* These three new works were not written with any plans for performance in mind but are instead "fictional performances" designed "to complete and make contemporary the ideas of this book."[6]

In the decades between Yamashita's exploration of Japan–United States relations in works like *GiLArex* and *Tokyo Carmen vs. L.A. Carmen* and the preparation of the collection *Anime Wong: Fictions of Performance,* global economics and politics changed dramatically. Yamashita felt it necessary to update the volume to represent these shifts. As Sohn describes, "Though Japan's economic primacy has since waned, the arc of this collection reveals how techno-Orientalism itself becomes reconfigured. In this vein, *Jan Ken Pon* spotlights China's new leadership role in the global economy and increasing Western fears that this change signals a potentially dangerous power shift in the Asia-Pacific."[7] Similarly, the piece entitled *Anime Wong: A CyberAsian Odyssey* updates techno-Orientalism for the early aughts to riff on Ronald A. Moore's hit remake of *Battlestar Galactica,* which featured a "cylon," a robot with artificial intelligence and awareness, played by the Korean American actress Grace Park. But the volume is more than just a critique of sci-fi tropes; it provides a rough-hewn introduction to Yamashita's ongoing themes: the benefits and dangers of cultural preservation as a community value, mainstream media's reductive depictions of Asian Americans, the roles technology and capitalism play in alienating people from their communities, and the dislocations experienced by transnational migrants. These different threads are woven together in fascinating, if sometimes confusing, ways. Yamashita riffs on familiar texts in order to emphasize the complex relationships between nationality, race, and geography. As in her novels, Yamashita is most interested in the social limbo that minorities and migrants inhabit.

Accordingly, the volume merits serious consideration for the role these performance pieces played in Yamashita's artistic development. The process of writing these performance works was both formative and transformative. As Yamashita observed in the acknowledgments to *Anime Wong,* "In the years I worked with performance, theater was for me a communal process and practice. Folks came together, created an event for a larger community. . . . A flat text on the page stood up and became voluminous, a wild beast, never entirely tamable, and this was exhilarating and dangerous. So many creative people devoted their time and risked their passions to be there, taming the beast" (389). Through her collaborative work with other Asian American female performance artists, Yamashita developed a wider vocabulary and repertoire for nontextual genres like dance and music, upon which she drew for her subsequent formal experimentations in fiction.

Formal and Historical Context

Just as she credits her husband with the conceptual ideas for *Through the Arc of the Rain Forest* and *Tropic of Orange,* Yamashita attributes her interest in theater to "the creative and endless imagination of Ronaldo Lopes de Oliveira . . . It was your traveling and work with the Brazilian theater groups Pão e Circo and Teatro Oficina, that edgy experience of inventing and innovating a stage almost literally from detritus, oil cans, and light bulbs at the back of an old automotive repair shop in São Paulo. For you, the possibilities for theater were provocative, makeshift, and slightly mad. You brought all that to L.A." (391). The low-budget, ad hoc, trial-and-error method of her theater collaborations was a crucible for working out new ideas. These invaluable experiences across various performance mediums gave Yamashita greater confidence to unleash her already formidable creativity even further. In the process, she crystallized her distinctive voice as a novelist who stretches the boundaries of realistic representation to capture the teeming, contradictory complexity of racial capitalism in the late twentieth and early twenty-first centuries.

As Yamashita noted, Asian and Asian American theater and dance forms were having a moment in the mid-1980s when she and her family relocated to Los Angeles. Inspired by the innovations she witnessed as an audience member, Yamashita recalled, "I wanted to somehow infuse Asian American theater with new work—with collaborative multi-media technologies thrown in with found detritus—that sort of postmodern future/past in which the primitive snuggles with the modern and progressive."[8] Suddenly it was possible to imagine writing for an Asian American audience, which opened up new avenues for formal experimentation, such as multilingual wordplay, adaptations of Japanese theater traditions, and layered intertextual references to Asian American literature and history.

Another key influence in this period was performance art, particularly work being done by Latin American and Latino artists exploring and commenting on the history of colonization in the Americas. The experimental art of solo performers like Guillermo Gómez-Peña and Luis Alfaro sparked new ideas for including technologies like video and slide projections that could critically engage with American history. She explained, "I had seen some of this in Brazil, and I wanted to bring that kind of challenge to a new theater experience. But, I wanted to do this in these newly minted institutions of Asian American theater."[9] One recognizes the extravagant theatricality and pointed political critique of Yamashita's imagination in her subsequent novels, such as *Tropic of Orange,* with its temporal-spatial "HyperContexts" tracking the global movements of people, or *I Hotel*'s impersonations of different genres to examine the limitations and possibilities of the yellow power movement.

Formally, Yamashita's performances are omnivorous, drawing on both Western and Japanese theatrical traditions, ranging from Bertholt Brecht and European opera to Noh and butoh. She seems to have embraced Brecht's idea of the *Verfremdungseffekt,* the alienation (alternatively translated as estrangement or distancing) effect, which seeks to engage audiences intellectually in order to stimulate social change, rather than to lull them into passive states of absorption. This is evident in her rewriting of canonical European operas, such as her doubling of Georges Bizet's *Carmen* to explore the dislocations of transnational migrants in *Tokyo Carmen vs. L.A. Carmen,* or her desire to recreate Giacomo Puccini's final *Madama Butterfly* aria in chicken clucks in "Madama B." She also found inspiration in Japanese theatrical forms including Kabuki, Noh, and butoh, which have their own distinct traditions of abstraction and artifice. Sohn notes that "many performance fictions in this collection address anxieties over ethnic preservation and purity by making clear that Japanese theater and performance modes . . . cannot be exported exactly into an American context."[10] Yamashita usually combines Anglo-European and Japanese performance forms in an uneasy balance designed to emphasize all that is and isn't translatable from one language to another, one culture to another, or one time to another. These combinations theatricalize incommensurability and loss, even as they teem with humorous observations about life as it is lived by contemporary Asian American men and women.

Not only are the individual performance pieces in *Anime Wong* experimental, but with its formal variation and dialectical engagement between text and archival material, the volume itself has all the hallmarks of Yamashita's genre-exploding novels. Indeed, as A. Robert Lee describes, the collection "steers nicely between reading text and play text, pieces equally to be met with by eye and hand while at the same time clearly intended for the stage, with directions supplied by Yamashita as to stage design and choreography, costume, and acoustics."[11] With its formal bravado and incorporation of visual and material records, the work bridges Yamashita's explorations of genre in *I Hotel* and her self-reflexive exploration of family/community history in *Letters to Memory* (2017). And yet, as a record of nearly three decades of writing and thinking, the volume is not as coherent or satisfying as either of those late-career works. Instead, *Anime Wong* is valuable for students and scholars for the ways it captures Yamashita's questing curiosity, her willingness to try new things and explore ideas that run counter to mainstream culture.

Cultural Preservation: *Kusei* and *GiLArex*

Anime Wong opens with *Kusei: Endangered Species* (1986), which was written by Yamashita with her husband Ronaldo Lopes de Oliveira and video artist Karen Mayeda, who also served as director and producer. This was later turned into a short film based on the script, partially funded by grants from the National Endowment for the Arts Expansion Arts Program and Video Communication's Filmmaker Development Program. Set in the year 2244, *Kusei* tells the story of a team of alien scientists who seek to save Japanese American culture from extinction by breeding an accidentally frozen third-generation Japanese American teenage girl from 1994, crowned "Miss Gardena" in a local pageant, with a clone of her childhood friend Kenji, identified as 805.AJA. Cultural preservation is thus imagined as a feat of technology, both unintentional (the young beauty queen was accidentally preserved in the freezer section of a grocery story after an extinction event) and deliberate (cloning). As she does throughout her career, Yamashita engages here in elaborate wordplay. Sohn describes the title as "an approximate Japanese pun, referring to something putrid or stinky (*kusai*), and is an offshoot of the word *kyusei,* a Japanese term denoting the ninth generation."[12] The title thus suggests that preserving the past is like the process of pickling: it prevents decomposition but brings its own funk.[13]

805.AJA is the last Japanese American male in the universe and the sole survivor from an alien planet named Topanzanar where the Japanese American bloodline was kept pure during the "Ford-Mitsubishi Wars." In imagining an alien planet named Topanzanar Yamashita draws on the history of Japanese American internment—Topaz and Manzanar were the names of two of the camps in which Japanese Americans on the West Coast were incarcerated after the bombing of Pearl Harbor—in order to examine racial "purity" as a consequence of exile and exclusion. Yamashita thus explores the logic of racial Othering that is also a tool for cultural preservation. The alien scientists' goal is to maintain "the cultural mixtures of two races without being threatening to either" (11). The impossibility of "cultural mixture" without risk or loss is the intellectual heart of the work. Indeed, if the only way to maintain ethnic culture is through isolation, imprisonment, or banishment, the cost is simply too high.

Moreover, in imagining a second Japanese internment located off-world as a result of a trade war between American and Japanese automotive companies, *Kusei* comments on the virulent racism and xenophobia of the 1980s, when white Americans feared rising Japanese economic and technological power. In 1982 Vincent Chin, a young Chinese American man celebrating his bachelor party in a Detroit suburb, was beaten to death by two white auto workers angry about layoffs due to increasing competition from Japanese automakers. Capitalism survives by dividing the laboring classes of different races and nationalities, rather than uniting them in common purpose against their overlords. Yamashita's concern with the detrimental role of capitalism in shaping geopolitics would be further explored in *Through the Arc of the Rain Forest* and *Tropic of Orange.*

Kusei is also noteworthy for its sly commentary on anthropology, as the alien scientists interpret their Japanese American subjects' every behavior as evidence of ethnic cultural patterns. Suggesting Yamashita's own reservations about the voyeurism of the discipline in which she was trained, the two Japanese American specimens are effectively collected like museum objects alongside other artifacts of twentieth-century Japanese American culture. When 805.AJA beats a taiko drum in the observation room, the clone's movements are absurdly attributed to "the beginning of the mating ritual" (11). Yamashita's concern with the ways in which scientific and social science discourses can reinscribe racism is further explored in *Jan Ken Pon.*

Interwoven into its examination of the dangers of cultural preservation as an absolute value, *Kusei* establishes one of Yamashita's ongoing thematic concerns in her theatrical work: conventional—that is to say, white—standards of beauty. *Kusei*'s lead female is a beauty queen and a cheerleader, a paragon of mainstream gender expectations for women. She is as insipid as one expects of a nineteen-year-old beauty pageant contestant remembered for being voted "best looking" by her high school classmates and earning a "B+ average" (9). She speaks in meaningless platitudes, as when she opines to her unseen pageant judges, "I hope to newly begin my struggles toward the peace and prosperity of mankind, and the universe" (7). Of course, the only kind of work to help "mankind" and "the universe" that is expected or desired of her is reproductive. *Kusei* ends when Queen drives off with 805.AJA in a 1986 Toyota convertible, charmed by his "rad car" and physical similarity to a boy from her youth (15). The alien scientists congratulate themselves for "retriev[ing] the species from extinction" (16). This dubious achievement is further undermined by the scientists' admission that the Queen's memory will soon be erased and "her brain will be a sociocultural vacuum" ready for reprogramming. The Japanese American woman is treated as an empty vessel or a blank slate whose value is in the service of isolationist reproduction; Asian American people become objects to be reproduced like widgets on an assembly line. *Kusei* thus suggests that "cultural preservation" comes at the expense of continued growth, development, and new experiences. Like other contemporary ethnic American writers such as Maxine Hong Kingston and Sherman Alexie, Yamashita insists that "cultural identity" is not a static, stable substance that continues unchanged from generation to generation. It is, instead, something alive and mutable, transformed by individual and group experiences over time.

The subject of cultural preservation is further explored *in GiLArex,* also performed as *GiLAwrecks,* and originally titled *Godzilla Comes to Little Tokyo* (1989), which was Yamashita's first fully produced musical. Vicki Abe composed the music, Yamashita wrote the story, and the two shared credit on song lyrics. The winner of the Northwest Asian American Theater's first annual playwright's contest, it was performed in Seattle at NWAAT in 1992. That same year, *GiLArex* was also given a staged reading at the Japanese American Cultural and Community Center (JACCC) in Los Angeles on August 21st and 23rd. *GiLArex* shows Yamashita's mature voice developing, and she brings increasing complexity to her signature themes. *GiLArex* combines her interest in media stereotypes of Asian American men and women with an exploration of the dangers of gentrification and urban development, which displace whole communities and have catastrophic effects on the environment. More narratively driven than her earlier theater work, *GiLArex* introduces Manzanar Murakami and Emi Yamane. Manzanar is a homeless Japanese American man who "conducts" Los Angeles traffic via an overpass. Since the play did not get further life onstage, Yamashita "wanted to resurrect this character," so he took on a major role in *Tropic of Orange.*[14] In *GiLArex* Emi is a fifteen-year-old with "no Japanese identity" who runs away from home and meets Manzanar. (In *Tropic of Orange,* Emi is reconceived as older, better informed, far more cynical about identity, and actually Manzanar's granddaughter.) Yamashita also recycles Ichiro, Jiro, and Saburo Terada from *Brazil-Maru,* transforming them into the Serizawa Brothers, Japanese businessmen and secret ninjas. Other characters include Emi's absentee father, Gary Yamane, an accomplished paleontologist "with a sense of the Earth's past but no personal cultural past"; Dr. Eugene Kirkpatrick, an anti-Japanese expert on the Pacific Rim; and various opinionated community activists who present competing ideas about one's obligation to maintain cultural traditions (75).

The work builds on the idea of the eventual extinction of Japanese Americans, which Yamashita explored in *Kusei.* Emi is "a cultural orphan" entirely estranged from Japanese American culture; she does not even recognize Japanese food (90). Sally Ogata is an active member of the Japanese America

Preservation League, whose "purpose is to find and preserve Japanese Americans," who "are a very rare species" (89–90). Sally's vision of preservation, however, is also problematic, as she wants to "pickle" Japanese American culture as it was several generations ago; fittingly, she dies trying to save the internment camp historical marker when the eponymous monster awakens from his prehistoric slumber beneath the desert floor. Sally is herself a kind of "dinosaur" obsessed with saving the past at the expense of ensuring the future.

And yet, *GiLArex* also considers the dangers of erasing the past in the pursuit of so-called progress. Yamashita plays with the metaphors of memory as a form of fossilization that records the past but can also lead to calcification. Emi is a sixth-generation Japanese American or *rokusei* (which she pronounces rock-say) who knows nothing of her own family history, let alone that of the Japanese American community. Her ignorance, like her father's lack of interest, is a kind of hardheadedness that threatens to destroy the beautiful aspects of their familial and cultural history. Emi and Gary sing a duet entitled "the Fossils of Our Past" that asks "But can our feelings take / the pressure of ions [sic] of time? / And who will then read / these fossils of leaf and fish? / The delicate imprints of our lives? / The delicate imprints of our love?" (123). Is memory too fragile a thing to survive the intense forces of time? These questions about the duty to remember and the costs to those who bear the burden of memory are explored by Yamashita with tremendous depth and feeling in *Letters to Memory* (2017).

The subject of cultural memory is also depicted via the relentless redevelopment of Los Angeles. In *GiLArex* the mayor teams up with the Serizawa brothers, Japanese real estate developers, to build the L.A. Colossus, a multiuse convention center and entertainment complex in the airspace above L.A.'s highways that promises to be "the most technically sophisticated and futuristic creation ever built anywhere in the world" (95). Yamashita satirizes such overhyped promises that disguise the workings of neoliberal global capitalism to privatize natural resources like air and water at devastating costs to ordinary citizens.

Similarly, Yamashita updates the Godzilla character, who was originally imagined as the product of genetic mutations caused by the atomic bombs that the United States military dropped on Japan during World War II. GiLArex is "a hybrid creature descended from both the Asian and American continents, a sort of Asian American dinosaur" who reemerges from under the Manzanar concentration camp as a result of a mixed-use redevelopment project (118). The eponymous monster represents late twentieth-century Japanese American traumas, including the cultural losses occasioned by Japanese internment and the environmental effects of overdevelopment. GiLArex wreaks havoc all over

L.A. but all he wants is to go back home to the Cretaceous period, when the ecosystem was in balance (138). Mysteriously, Manzanar's conducting keeps the monster calm, and, like the pied piper, he leads GiLArex back to the Owens Valley, destroying an aqueduct and bringing water back to the desert. The land is returned to its original state, the monster drowns, and Los Angelenos are reawakened to human connection by the necessity to get out of their cars and actually talk to one another.[15] Rad Man and Lovely Lady, who have been locked in a perpetual flirtation on their daily commutes, finally meet in person amid rubble on the freeway. Once the environmental order is restored (and the techno-capitalist gentrification project is dead), love can bloom in the desert. The work thus presages the cautious optimism of *Tropic of Orange,* which imagines the creation of an alternative social order in Los Angeles after the freeway is stopped.

Racial and Gender Stereotypes

The majority of the texts in *Anime Wong: Fictions of Performance* deal with the deleterious effects that media images have on Asian American men and women's relationships and identities. As in many of her performance works, Yamashita's goal is to defamiliarize conventional representations of Asia and Asian America in order to highlight their artificiality and emphasize white people's limited recognition of the full range of Asian American experiences.

Hannah Kusoh: An American Butoh (1988) continued Yamashita's fruitful collaboration with other Asian American women artists. Vicki Abe wrote music, Shizuko Hoshi served as choreographer and director, and Mayeda created videos and slide projections. (Yamashita's husband helped with set design and lighting.) The work premiered at the Japanese American Cultural and Community Center in Los Angeles as part of their "Fresh Tracks" contemporary performance series September 9–10, 1989, where it was billed as "an imaginative mad brainstorm of four Japanese American female artists."[16] It was performed again at Highways performance space in Santa Monica March 28–30, 1990. The work is pointedly experimental and political, exploring beauty standards and stereotypes of Asian American women through six senses: smell, touch, sight, taste, sound, and intuition (the "sixth sense"). *Hannah Kusoh* combines various forms of expression (music, dance, videos/slide projections, narration, and dialogue). As is true of her fiction, Yamashita's theatrical performances are animated by verbal dexterity and play with language; as she explains, *hanakuso* means "boogers, the detritus that emerges from your nose."[17] The play opens with videos of the atomic bomb being detonated and images of Japanese internment, accompanied by acrid scents wafted at the audience. As Yamashita recalled, "We had a hot wok on stage, and someone would throw a tablespoon of teriyaki sauce on it and filled the theater with that burnt smell. We also opened jars of Japanese pickles that smell like fart . . . . We wanted that sort of visceral experience."[18] (Clearly Yamashita has a fascination with the olfactory experience.) Shifting between lighthearted irony and serious critique, the work created a provocative and not always pleasant theatrical experience that asks, are real Asian American women, who fail to live up to stereotypes, the detritus of the title? Or are stereotypes the disgusting, abject objects that need to be expelled?

The work emphasizes the hybridity of real-life Asian American women, an idea reinforced formally and thematically, as is evident from the opening stage direction about music, which requires "mixed cultural instruments: koto, shakuhachi, marimba, bagpipes, or some other sansei invention of a multicultural nature" (25). Such forms of cultural hybridity are interwoven with familiar scenes of Western Orientalism, such as the Chinese dance from *The Nutcracker Suite* and Gilbert and Sullivan's *The Mikado*. *Hannah Kusoh* also draws on the Japanese dance form of butoh, which was developed by Hijikata Tatsumi in Tokyo in the late 1960s and early 1970s. Butoh typically involves near-naked dancers with white face and body paint moving with deliberate, contorted movements as a means to explore the human experience.[19] Yamashita's use of butoh formally amplifies her thematic concern with Asian American women's socially prescribed and proscribed behaviors; the art form was originally developed to delve into personal history "to break free of previous unconscious physical and mental strictures."[20] Similarly, *Hannah Kusoh* considers the various influences that shape contemporary Asian American women's identity in California and investigates how to liberate oneself from the weight of cultural expectations and stereotypes.

The work features videos of a sansei woman "discussing her blind date with a Japanophile" who treats her like an exotic object to be added to his collection (26).[21] For Asian American women, the fetishization of Japan by white men with "yellow fever" is a blunt instrument for identity erasure. The woman in the video is only seen as an exotic, erotic object by white men, while she explains that in reality, "the only things Japanese about me are my name and my eyes" (29). Of course, those external features are all that men like those who date her care about. On the subject of vision, actors recite literary quotations about eyes alongside medical quotations describing the surgery that can create a European-looking "double eyelid." *Hannah Kusoh* makes the audience uncomfortable by juxtaposing familiar, even clichéd quotations about the beauty and soulfulness of eyes with reminders of the costs of achieving Western-style beauty for Asian women. Achieving "natural beauty" can be a very painful and unnatural process.

Hannah Kusoh is full of ideas, but it reads as overly complicated and it is hard to imagine the work being executed effectively on stage. The *LA Times* dismissed *Hannah Kusoh* as "a slick, lightweight, collaborative revue touching on the frustrations of being a young, banal, middle-class Japanese American woman in Los Angeles today."[22] While that harsh verdict clearly comes from the position of a white male dismissing the theatricalization on stage of the underrepresented experiences of Asian American women, the work does come off now as altogether too didactic. As the program for the JACCC performance spells out, *Hannah Kusoh* "exposes the often cruel stereotyping of Japanese American women" (51). The work suffers from its tendency to "tell" rather than "show" its message to audiences, thereby reducing its emotional impact. Like many of Yamashita's performance works, this one presents a series of parodic skits or character types rather than a unified narrative of emotional depth. There is a deliberate cartoonish quality to many of these texts, with everything exaggerated and comical.

In *Tokyo Carmen vs. L.A. Carmen* (1990), Yamashita examines the asymmetries of racial privilege and sexual fetishization across two continents. Yamashita again teamed up with Hoshi and Mayeda for this work; scenery was created by Lopes de Oliveira and Chris Tashima. The story is a retelling of Georges Bizet's opera *Carmen* on Japanese American themes. Yamashita has an abiding interest in opera, both in terms of interrogating its history of Orientalism (*Madama Butterfly, The Mikado*) and creating her own contemporary Japanese American versions of these plots. *Tokyo Carmen vs. L.A. Carmen* was performed at the Taper, Too in Los Angeles for three nights in June 1990, as part of the 13th Hour project to produce new works by emerging performance artists. In an *LA Times* review, the play was lauded for being the "weirdest and wildest of all" the performances and praised for its "splendidly deadly caricatures" of American and Japanese executives in an "eye-popping, fast-moving piece."[23] Once again Yamashita fuses disparate styles: old and new, Japanese and Euro-American, cartoonish and realistic. She specifically instructs that costumes and makeup be "Butoh in style, flamboyant mixtures of flamenco, Gypsy, and yakuza (body tattooing and so on, satin blood reds and blacks" (163). The music is played on a similar mixture of instruments: flamenco guitar, shamisen, saxophone, and taiko drum.

There are two Carmens here, one in Tokyo and one in Los Angeles. The former is a white American who wants to join an all-female "Japanese Rockette troupe called the Takarazuka" (178); the latter is a Japanese geisha who moved to L.A. to become a flamenco dancer. Both Carmens are in thrall to the yakuza. The other roles from Bizet's opera are likewise doubled into "L.A." and "Tokyo" versions. *Tokyo Carmen vs. L.A. Carmen* features four actors, each of whom plays two parts. L.A. Carmen is romantically involved with Jiro, a Japanese samurai-turned-salaryman working in L.A., and Ebizo, a famous Kabuki actor relocated to Hollywood to play bit parts on television. According to Yamashita's staging, both male roles are to be played by the same Asian actor. Tokyo Carmen is involved with Joe, a white American car salesman in Tokyo to start a new business, and Skipper, a white American pitcher who plays baseball for a Japanese team; both of these male roles are to be performed by the same white actor. The same Asian actress who performs L.A. Carmen is also expected to play Maki, Jiro's wife who is unhappy in L.A. and longs to return to Japan to start a family. The white actress who performs Tokyo Carmen also plays Michele, Joe's wife who wants to return to L.A. to build her career.[24]

Crucially, each love triangle is intra-racial: the Tokyo triad are all Americans living in Japan, while the L.A. triad are all Japanese who feel out of place in the United States. The play ends as Bizet's opera does, with each Carmen murdered by one lover (Jiro/Joe) when she is on the verge of choosing the other (Ebizo/Skipper). But Yamashita combines that story with a modified version of the *Madama Butterfly* plot, having the jilted wife (Maki/Michele) commit suicide. (In Puccini's opera, it is the American wife who keeps the man and the geisha who dies by suicide.) By doubling the characters and combining two plots, Yamashita defamiliarizes two iconic European operas. Through its transnational comparisons, *Tokyo Carmen vs. L.A. Carmen* examines the asymmetries of racial privilege and sexual fetishization across two continents.

For example, when Tokyo Carmen (who is white) recounts how she was recruited to Japan under false pretenses, she makes clear that her race and gender were both desirable and exploitable: "Sure I was supposed to dance, but I was supposed to dance with Japanese men who would pay good money to dance with a white woman. Then you begin to get the picture—it wasn't just dancing they wanted." But she reveals her own racist attitudes when she goes on to describe "all these horny little Japanese men [who] were trying to get some white ass" (178). Provocatively, Yamashita explores the gender dynamics of all her characters, with the men struggling to perform their roles as breadwinners and avatars of national masculinity, while their wives—unmoored from the work or family lives that provide them their identities back home—feel unable to define themselves as anything other than helpmeets to the men. The Carmens are sexually dominated by men, from the gangsters who control their businesses and bodies to the lovers who are supposed to rescue them but become their murderers instead. As the Carmens say, "It's a man's world" (177). Unlike a work like *Miss Saigon* (1989), which updated *Madama Butterfly* to depict the American war in Vietnam as a tragic interracial romance, *Tokyo Carmen vs. L.A. Carmen* actually adds complexity to the source material, highlighting the multiple axes of power among its characters and critiquing the ideologies that allow for such inequalities. All of the characters seem unable to break out of their assigned racial-gender roles: the women are either sexual sirens or jilted wives, while the men are emasculated husbands or racial mascots.

It is important to acknowledge that Yamashita updates her source text to underscore the complex relationships between nationality, race, and geography in Japan and the United States. As the opening/overture notes explain, these characters "are people in transit, temporary visitors, temporarily putting off the real plans of their lives to be in foreign environments" (169). As in so much of her writing, Yamashita is interested in the cultural no-man's-land between two countries. She is not interested in immigrant assimilation into a new home nation; rather, she considers the social limbo of feeling not at home and being unable to imagine one's new location as ever becoming home. Jiro is "lost in America, in a country where, even after two years, he cannot speak English." Likewise, Joe "is lost in Japan, in a country where, even after two years, he can hardly speak Japanese" (165, 167). Ebizo, though a famous Kabuki actor in Japan, struggles to make a career in Los Angeles, where he can only find work in "stereotypical roles in commercials," suggesting the ways American racism limits his success (165). Skipper, a benchwarmer in the United States, does find success and popularity as an American baseball player in Japan, but he is a kind of exotic token. Both of their wives are miserable as socially invisible plus-ones in foreign countries. None of these characters have taken root in their transplanted environments.

As she does in greater detail in *Circle K Cycles,* Yamashita depicts the dislocations of transient workers and the contrasts between locales as expressions of cultural differences. To the Japanese couple, L.A. feels oversize and impersonal: Maki describes living "in this big American house in Torrance. I should be grateful. There are four bedrooms and three bathrooms and a big living room, big kitchen, big washing machine, big dishwasher, and giant refrigerator . . . I have a big American car to go to the Giant supermarket. I should be very happy" (170). Conversely, in Tokyo the Americans feel claustrophobic; Michele complains, "I never thought I'd ever be living in such an itty bitty house; everywhere you turn, you bump into something. The bathroom is so small you can only take a bath if you close this door, but you can't use the toilet unless you open the door . . . Out there it's wall-to-wall Japanese" (171). Yamashita emphasizes this contrast via her staging, which places each woman inside comic-book-style panels: "Maki is bordered by very large borders, which seem to make her distant and small, while Michele is squeezed between borders (sometimes as small as her face or lips), having to press on them and struggle to talk within very small confines" (170). Yamashita does not take advantage of the stage so much as she seems to want to transform it back into the page to reinforce the work's themes.

For all its literary engagement with European opera, *Tokyo Carmen vs. L.A. Carmen* is equally committed to historicizing global economics in the late 1980s. The work features a scene in Act II where all four actors elucidate a "list of trade imbalance statements" between the United States and Japan, expressing racial nationalism through trade war propaganda:

> America has shoddy merchandise.
> Japan is a racist country.
> America is a racist country.
> Japanese consumers subsidize their foreign markets.
> The yen is overvalued.
> The dollar has lost its strength.
> The Japanese are buying up downtown L.A.
> America for Americans.
> Japan for Japanese. (175)

Yamashita suggests that operatic themes of love and betrayal may be universal, but historical context matters. Accordingly, in the 1980s-set world of *Tokyo Carmen vs. L.A. Carmen,* national masculinity is represented not by soldiers and bullfighters but by culture workers (actor, baseball player) and desk jockeys desperately trying to preserve their sense of authority in a changing world.

Like *Tokyo Carmen,* the short story "Madama B" (1993) plays with iconic Western opera to question influential depictions of Asian and Asian American womanhood in popular culture. Cheekily subtitled "based on a true story," "Madama B" is a comic narrative about a chicken named after the tragic figure. While the work is not a performance piece, it had its genesis in theater and is connected thematically to other works in the collection. The story begins with Yamashita wanting to capture the sound of a chicken singing the final, tragic aria from Puccini's *Madama Butterfly* as part of a collaboration with Vicki Abe during the years Yamashita worked as a secretary. Yamashita describes her aim: "The idea was to synthesize the song of a chicken and to reproduce the sound operatically. The bright performance proposal was to have Puccini's famous aria sung by a chicken" (61). Yamashita seeks to show the artificiality and incongruity of Puccini's fantasy version of Asian womanhood through the discordant sound of a chicken "singing" the renowned aria. What follows is a comedy of errors as Yamashita brings home the bird and attempts to record its squawking.

This irreverent approach to tragic opera is quintessential Yamashita, mocking the self-seriousness and Orientalism of the Western operatic tradition through parodic homage. What begins as a wacky idea becomes a kind of quixotic quest. Once she gets the chicken, all plans for a quick recording and a delicious dinner are set aside when her children grow attached to the bird. But Madama B will not make the requisite sounds, much like Yamashita herself does not live up to the stereotype of the ideal Japanese American. She describes her own backyard as a delightful place for her children to explore, but "nothing is pruned or cultivated or even remotely like a Japanese American garden. It's truly an embarrassment to my upbringing. Not that we don't have plans, but for now, our house is a Hollywood set; only the front has the aspect of suburban cultivation" (68). Yamashita and her chicken both resist expectations to perform on cue as others expect them to behave. They follow their own idiosyncratic rhythms.

Madama B eventually lays eggs that hatch into little chicks, and Yamashita successfully records her sounds, but she cannot let go of her pet. Her friends and family fail to understand the purpose of the project, to see how the chicken connects to Puccini's opera. She insists, "This is abstract theater! This is satire! This is the point at which a chicken meets technology. I think about Madama B, the chicken, staring with one eye at the recorder in silence. Now what was that opera again? A Japanese woman kills herself because her white lover leaves. The chicken stares at the recorder with her other eye. Yeah, so what is it?" (70). The art takes on a life of its own, with meaning far beyond its initial intention as parody. Later, she rehomes the chicken on a farm, and a week later the performance finally occurs. For all the drama of its production, "The chicken aria is just one piece in the entire performance, one obsessive, decadent, avant-garde moment, obscured by video and slide images, lights and writhing dancers. Tienti la tuapaura, io con sicurafede lo aspetto. Some people mistake it for a broken disk drive. A byte of sound" (71).[25] Tragedy blends into comedy, fantasy meets reality, nature meets technology. Yamashita mocks the racialized and gendered projections of Euro-American opera, while highlighting the messy, comical beauty of her own real-life modern Asian American nuclear and artistic families.

In 1992 Yamashita was awarded a City of Los Angeles Cultural Grant, which helped support development of *Noh Bozos: A Circus Performance* (1993), a companion piece to *Hannah Kusoh* that examines the stereotypes that oppress Asian American men. Written by Yamashita, directed by Hoshi, choreographed by Mimosa (the daughter of Hoshi and Mako), featuring music composed by Glenn Horiuchi and sets designed by Lopes de Oliveira, *Noh Bozos* mixes elements of Japanese Noh theater with the American circus and sideshow in a ten-act structure.[26] Originating in the fourteenth century, Noh is a highly stylized, ritualized Japanese musical dance form "that is fundamentally non-realistic." It originally featured male actors performing in symbolic carved masks and costumes, accompanied by a chorus and instrumental music.[27] Noh is characterized by small, tightly choreographed movements, a fitting form for Yamashita's exploration of the narrow roles for Asian American men. Instead of traditional depictions of gods and heroes, Yamashita's *Noh Bozos* explores Japanese American celebrities who are presented as exhibits in a "live freak show." It features satiric depictions of a variety of Los Angeles Asian American male types, such as local politicians (Warren Furutani, Norman Mineta, Robert Matsui, and Michael Woo), martial artists from popular culture (Karate Kid, Teenage Mutant Ninja Turtles, and Bruce Lee), sansei salarymen slogging away at middle-management jobs, and a pregnant version of David Henry Hwang's cross-dressing M. Butterfly (251).[28] It was given three shows at the JACCC in Los Angeles in August 1993. In 1996, it was performed as a staged reading at Theater Mu, an Asian American theater company in Minneapolis, as part of their "New Eyes Festival" showcasing Asian American writers.

Noh Bozos is a comic and futuristic work in which sansei men are an endangered species who experience constant, casual racism. Much as *Hannah Kusoh* examines standards of beauty for Asian American women, *Noh Bozos* taxonomizes different Asian American male "types": the "Gardena Bro," the "Westside Dude," the "Eastside Homeboy," and the "Valley Boy" (206). These men inhabit "sansei limbo," which "is a murky, undefined space between the Westside and the Eastside, between Gardena and the Valley. Somewhere in the middle, the struggle for culture continues" (207). The muddled middle is where cultural hybridity is most manifest. Underscoring this theme, Yamashita describes musicians combining Japanese and American instruments, and mixing classical Japanese and American jazz compositions. Yamashita's stage notes indicate that "there is both the festive air of a circus and the solemn air of a Noh ceremony" (203). Yamashita thus suggests the comedy and tragedy of cultural stereotyping.

In *Noh Bozos* Yamashita also explores racism and cultural nationalism through her depictions of doubles and doppelgängers. *Noh Bozos* features two sansei men, one working for an American company and the other for a Japanese company, both of whom are stuck at middle management. Yamashita highlights the intersectional nature of anti-Asian racism by literalizing their barriers to success with the feminized image of the "glass ceiling." One is a perpetual overachiever, the other a B+ student, but both are continually overlooked for promotion. Similarly, the play closes with a duet between an Asian American woman and an Asian American man on a first date; they don't find each other attractive because each has internalized mainstream American cultural ideas about sexual attractiveness; he desires Dolly Parton and she wants Dennis

Quaid. While Asian American men and women face similar issues, Yamashita shows how they internalize white supremacy separately. The couple's failure to connect is both funny and sad.

For the volume *Anime Wong: Fictions of Performance,* Yamashita updates the stereotypes she analyzed in the previously discussed works in an unproduced performance piece titled *Anime Wong: A CyberAsian Odyssey* (2008). The title is a verbal play on the legendary Asian American actress of early cinema Anna May Wong. Here Anime Wong is a larger-than-life superstar/goddess/android embodying a range of Asian American stereotypes. The work *AW* (as the play is referred to here, to avoid confusion with the volume title) continues Yamashita's exploration of technology in relation to Asian American history and identity. Focusing on film and television representations from the 1970s to the 2010s, Yamashita revises her earlier theater work for the twenty-first century.

AW is organized as six separate "Mangas," with a commercial break in the middle to advertise a Japanese smart toilet. Each manga is like a mini-play with its own dramatis personae, location, sets, and costumes. Yamashita here loosely uses the term "manga" to denote a caricatured Asian and Asian American cultural form. But her goal is to satirize mainstream American popular cultural representations of Asians. Manga I features the eponymous Anime Wong emerging from inside a giant Goddess of Democracy statue based on the Statue of Liberty, "looking like some kind of androgynous Asian Barbie with Anna May Wong makeup and hair and maybe a version of a *Thief of Baghdad* costume, the apron flap being the image of a Warhol Mao covering her hot pants" (295). This figure combines the accumulated imagery of old-fashioned Orientalism, techno-Orientalism, and the recent pageantry of the 2008 Beijing Olympics in order to represent the Orientalized future, also known as "the Matrix-archy!" (295). Yamashita thus highlights the fears and fantasies embodied in the slippage between alien and Asian in popular culture. Science fiction as a genre has long positioned the Other of the future as Asian, whether an alien from another planet or a man-made robot run amok. As Stephen Hong Sohn explains, "In its multiply inflected significations, the alien stands as a convenient metaphor for the experiences of Asian Americans, which range from the extraterrestrial being who seems to speak in a strange, yet familiar, accented English to the migrant subject excluded from legislative enfranchisement."[29] In popular culture, Asian-ness too often substitutes for inviolable difference against which a presupposed white humankind must measure itself.

Manga II examines the sexual power of the figure of the Asian/Alien via Yamashita's version of the story of Odysseus and the Sirens. Here the sirens are half-bird, half-human versions of the "cylons," the artificially intelligent robots of Ronald A. Moore's lauded reboot of *Battlestar Galactica,* who threaten

Anime Wong "and the whole CyberAsian crew" traveling to Angel Island, the port of entry for Asian immigrants to the West Coast of the United States in the nineteenth and early twentieth centuries (297). Using mock Japanglish, Yamashita emphasizes the cultural and aural similarities between sirens/cylons. In Moore's sci-fi universe, one of the cylons was played by Korean American actress Grace Park, in whose body the popular culture image of Asian/Alien woman as seductive destroyer of Western civilization, or perhaps its salvation, was made manifest. Likewise, Yamashita's sirens are "irresistible, seductive, provocative, gorgeous, most perfect" specimens (298). After Orpheus fails to save those on the ship with his lyre, Anime Wong survives by having sex with all of the cyborgs, while a Madame Butterfly cyborg has sex with a toaster. The Asian woman turns out to be the crew's savior through her combustive sexuality. Yamashita thus takes to absurd lengths the twin ideas of the erotic exotic Asian woman and of yellow peril fears of the alien (Asian) Other, which have shaped U.S. culture for nearly two centuries.

Manga III merges the alien hive-mind character the Borg from *Star Trek: The Next Generation,* who invades and assimilates its hosts, with the racist caricature of the Dragon Lady, played by the actress Anna May Wong in several early Fu Manchu films. Anime Wong transforms into one of the "BorgAsians" with "metal parts and heavy machinery that extends behind her in wings and claws," ominously intoning, "surrender your bodies. Your culture will adapt. Resistance is futile," while images of mixed-race people are projected on video screens (302). Through this iteration of Anime Wong Yamashita literalizes racist yellow peril discourse about Asia enforcing conformity. In contrast, Data, the yellow-skinned robot from *Star Trek: TNG,* appears as a figure for the gentle and nonthreatening model minority; this figure suggests that Asians are robotic and only pretending to behave like humans. The manga ends with Anime Wong and Data in a sexual embrace, alongside video screens announcing Anime Wong's seduction of various white actors and directors associated with techno-Orientalism: "Anime Wong sleeps with Ridley Scott! Anime Wong in steamy relationship with Harrison Ford! Anime Wong seen with new beau: Bruce Willis! Anime Wong in love with Will Smith!" (307). Yamashita suggests the realization of long-feared and/or desired sexual conquest of the West by the East in Hollywood science fiction.

A commercial break advertising the "iToto" "intelligent toilet"—it can be programmed to speak in a variety of Asian voices, from Yoda to Bruce Lee to Pikachu—interrupts the manga sequence. The toilet demands payment in the form of binaries: "East. West.; Technology. Culture.; Machines. Humans" (310). As with *Hannah Kusoh,* Yamashita satirizes dichotomous racial stereotypes as both valuable currency and flushable waste.

Manga IV features two Anime Wongs, representing the twin depictions of Evil vs. Good alien/Asian/cyborg. The alien/Asian/cyborg will either be the end of humanity or its savior, as embodied on one hand by monsters like Godzilla and the xenomorph from Ridley Scott's sci-fi film classic *Alien* (1979), and on the other hand by the virtuous humanoid robot Astro Boy. This chapter culminates in a battle (not unlike the battle between SUPERNAFTA and El Gran Mojado in *Tropic of Orange*) between "our techno-Oriental atomic robot/cyborg/android, programmed with a conscience, a sense of sacrifice and duty, and the will to save humanity, our global citizen: Little Boy Astro" and "that phallic-faced dinosaur, that supersized insect with its DNA programmed to survive, born out of great human evil but impervious to any knowledge of sin, our chest buster and global alien: Godzilla" (312–313). As the two Anime Wongs fight, they seem to destroy each other. Neither role offers a meaningful path to live in the world.

Manga V explores the contradictory fantasies of racialized gender roles as embodied by the Disney version of Mulan, the story of a female warrior who disguises herself as a man to save her family. Inverting David Henry Hwang's *M. Butterfly,* which was about a man who posed as a woman to gain power, manhood here becomes "just a matter of strategy and tactics" and is thus "based on deception" (314). Yamashita draws on long-standing stereotypes of the Asian man as not really a man, as well as of Asians as fundamentally duplicitous and treacherous, to show the stereotype of the Asian woman to be the most dangerous and deadly of all.

The final manga takes the idea of the female assassin further, combining the ritualized, Orientalized combat of Iron Chef and Quentin Tarantino's *Kill Bill: Vol. I* (2003). The reader encounters two versions of ass-kicking femininity, the "Bride" and the "Geisha." The Bride, like the namesake character played by Uma Thurman, represents white cultural appropriation of Asia, "probably all blonde, 007 babes, undercover spies, buffed-up bad girls"; the Geisha represents "any number of Asian women: Michelle Yeoh, Ziyi Zhang, Kelly Hu, Maggie Q, Grace Park, and other bungee-jumping Asian bad girls" (320). The "theme" for their culinary battle is China, with each combatant presenting one set of stereotypes about the country, embodying a range of yellow peril fears. The Bride's menu represents contemporary anxieties about China, embodied in her meal of "a delicate appetizer of dog food dumplings laced with melamine, followed by Severe Acute Respiratory Syndrome, or SARS, served as a centerpiece on a soft bed of juk" along with "an aspic of concentrated greenhouse gases." The Geisha's meal consists of "stuffed avian flu followed by a water torture broth with fried CIA documents . . . ending with the one-child policy seared and sliced and spread thinly on a multicolored Tibetan mandala" (323–324). As in the previous manga, the scenes end with the outcome uncertain. Who can "win" such scenarios? Everyone loses when the only options are dehumanizing stereotypes.

Anime Wong: A CyberAsian Odyssey clearly updates the gender and racial stereotypes Yamashita has explored her whole career in order to address early twenty-first-century geopolitics. Cleverly but exhaustingly invoking a huge variety of popular culture figures, the work's message risks becoming scattershot and diffuse. It is hard to see how this work would be accessible to any but the most devoted Yamashita fans or well-informed Asian American scholars. The effect is simultaneously muddled and bludgeoning, rather than keenly incisive.

Academic Metafictions: *Siamese Twins and Mongoloids* and *Jan Ken Pon*

Siamese Twins and Mongoloids: Three Abstractions on Asian America (2012) further explores stereotypes of Asian Americans throughout history and across genres, while also critiquing the ways that the institutionalization of Asian American studies in universities creates equally narrow forms of representation. The work is also concerned with Asian Americans' participation in toxic forms of masculinity. The final work in the collection, *Jan Ken Pon* (2012), takes aim at scientific disciplines that unwittingly reinscribe racial stereotypes and international competition, particularly around sex and money.

Siamese Twins and Mongoloids is a work in three parts, including a stage play, a television script, and a parody of *The Mikado*. The work was inspired by a project solicited by pioneering Asian American studies scholar Amy Ling. The first part of *Siamese Twins and Mongoloids* appears as a chapter in *I Hotel*, within the "1971: Aiiieeeee! Hotel" novella. Parts two and three were written in 2012.[30] The work's title suggests how Western culture has long associated Asia with disability, via now-obsolete racist terminology. Echoing *Noh Bozos* and its exploration of the narrow range of roles for Asian American subjects, Yamashita once again depicts an "Asian freak show" (264). Similarly, continuing her fascination with doubles and doppelgängers, "Abstraction 1: Dramatic Theater—*Hyphenated Dreams*" features five sets of conjoined (a.k.a. "Siamese") twins, the offspring of "a hapless outlaw," Sung Chiang, who poses as an ordinary Chinese laborer named Ah Gee. Pa wants to split each set of twins to give them a singular identity: "Come to America, and your children all come out hyphenated. Half this–half that. Nothing whole. Everything half-ass. And it's more complicated than that. One half trying to be the other half and vice versa. As they say, duking out the dialectics. Working through schizophrenia and assimilation" (264). The "search for Asian America" provokes anxiety, forcing an impossible choice between two "authentic" cultures that are not separate so much as unevenly combined (265).

To demonstrate this theme, each of the pairs of twins is a well-known popular culture duo featuring Asian or Asian American characters reduced to ethnic stereotypes or catchphrases in American popular culture: Charlie Chan and #1 Son, Mao and Confucius, Green Hornet and Kato, Captain Kirk and Mr. Zulu [sic], and Fu Manchu and Dragon Lady. In her half-formed theatrical vision, Yamashita admits that "the stage directions for representing Siamese twins are vague. Actors might share a pant leg or be drawn together in a constant embrace with appropriate costuming. Clever use of acrobatics might produce grotesquely comic attachments. This might be a director's nightmare, but the playwright insists on the visual possibilities of the circus—an Asian freak show. As I always say, it's best to use your imagination" (264). The theme of this first section is an exploration of the "split personalities" or "identity crisis" characteristic of life in "Asian America," where the only visible options in the media are sycophants, sidekicks, Oriental mystics, or yellow peril villains.

The work continues with "Abstraction 2: Television Sitcom—*Dentaloptics,*" which imagines a 1990s-set television show featuring conjoined twin brothers Heco and Okado Hamada, who are paragons of Asian American respectability, with stereotypical talents and interests. Heco is a dentist who plays taiko and shakuhachi, while Okada is an optometrist and "math genius" who practices sumi-e watercolor painting and calligraphy; both excel at martial arts. Both men are artistic, athletic, and logical, but in different ways that complement each other (266). They were raised "to epitomize, mentally and physically, the very perfection of Asian America" (269). But the two actually are undercover civil rights activists charged with stopping a real estate blockbusting conspiracy. Secondary plots include their omnicompetent and underappreciated secretary Lucy quitting the office to work for their father's political campaign, and Heco and Okada's appearance in a beefcake Asian American Male calendar, which scandalizes their father and threatens his reelection among his conservative constituents.[31] All ends well and order is restored in typical sitcom fashion. Heco and Okada manage to stop the racist real estate scheme, while showing Asian American men as sexy, and being loyal sons who help their father get reelected. "Abstraction 3" embodies the liberal fantasy that the model minority myth could be a convenient cover for more radical, coalition-based anti-racist activism, as well as a refutation of pernicious racial-gender stereotypes—without sacrificing more traditional cultural values such as filial piety.

"Abstraction 3: Opera—*Mike Kato*" riffs on the genre of opera by updating Gilbert and Sullivan's Orientalist fantasy *The Mikado* to comment on the stereotypes and complexities of contemporary Asian America. Yamashita's version features "Mike Kato" (that is, Mikado) as a professor of Asian American studies married to an activist attorney (Katisha). Mike and Katisha's daughter

Peep-Bo is a transnational adoptee from Korea. Kato is having an affair with a graduate student (Yum-Yum) who is herself in love with Kato's teaching assistant Nanki-Poo. Meanwhile, Yum-Yum's mother, Pitti-Sing, is having an affair with Katisha. Yamashita humorously updates the characters to reflect modern gender roles, sexualities, and Asian American politics. Each scene is similarly accompanied by mocking titles for imagined contemporary arias, such as *Google It, Based on a True Story,* and *Facebook for the Faceless.*

In a neat intertextual turn, Mike lectures his students on the television series described in the previous abstraction, which he describes as the only "successful Asian American sitcom that lasted three seasons and sixty-three episodes . . . It was our *Ozzie and Harriet,* our *Leave It to Beaver*" (282). Mike explains that the characters of Heco and Okada were based on Chang and Eng Bunker, the original "Siamese twins" who performed as human oddities for P. T. Barnum before settling in North Carolina, where they became genteel Southern plantation owners who owned slaves, fought for the Confederacy, and raised large families. *DentalOptics* transforms these twins into personifications of 1990s political correctness, complete with Heco marrying a Connie Chung look-alike and his brother wedding a woman who is "one quarter Cherokee, one quarter African American, one eighth Palestinian, and three eighths Micronesian" (283). The humor of this revision is lost on his young students, suggesting both the dryness of academic discourse and a deepening generation gap.[32]

The remainder of the third abstraction spins out Yamashita's update of the *Mikado* plot for twenty-first century audiences, including such plot points as a lesbian relationship, transnational adoption, "the Uyghur Chinese detained at Guantanamo Bay" after the September 11th terrorist attacks, and the emergence and ubiquity of Internet technologies like Skype and online porn. As the couples rearrange themselves into new romantic configurations, Nanki-Poo and his buddies Go-To and Pish-Tush dream of a future business venture that will help them conquer markets across Asia. The work ends with the screening of Mike's documentary film about the production of *DentalOptics.* Mike's film is praised, and Asian American celebrities fondly recall the sitcom and its influence. During the question and answer period, Ko-Ko, the Lord High Executioner, pulls out two assault weapons from his kimono.

Sohn interprets the ending as questioning "the institutionalization of ethnic studies: can it retain any coherent political vision, especially considering the heterogeneity of the Asian American population? Rather than reading this piece as a call to terminate the study of Asian Americans, Ko-Ko's provocative concluding stance instead suggests that we must be ever more vigilant against the forces that seek to dismantle it" (376). While Yamashita clearly is invested in and critical of the institutionalization of ethnic studies in the academy, the work's ending also responds to the crisis of masculinity in American culture more broadly. Yamashita is alluding to the troubling gun violence committed by American men, including those of Asian American descent—such as the half-Filipino Andrew Cunanan, who killed the fashion designer Gianni Versace in 1997, and Korean American Seung-Hui Cho, who killed fellow students and professors at Virginia Tech in 2007.[33] Asian Americans, despite widespread stereotypes of passivity and feminization, are not immune from the toxic masculinity of American culture. Indeed, those pernicious stereotypes provide dangerous fuel for retributive violence, as in the example of Elliot Rodger, who murdered six people in 2014 out of anger at his failure to attract women. Such darkness shadows the work's otherwise lighthearted tone, suggesting the dangers of failing to correct Hollywood images of Asian American masculinity.

The final new work in the collection is *Jan Ken Pon,* meaning, rock, paper, scissors, which, according to "the Asian American narrative" was brought by Japanese Americans to the United States. This work appears on the page as a PowerPoint presentation with notes, which functions like an abstracted, performative version of a lecture being given in a college classroom. Yamashita braids together Asian American history and debates about nature and nurture through the real-life work of Barry Sinervo, an evolutionary biologist at the University of California, Santa Cruz. Sinervo analogizes male side-blotch lizards in the Coast Range of California as engaged in a color-based version of rock-paper-scissors in order to assert dominance. Yamashita includes an extended conversation between Sinervo and a radio host, whereby readers learn that it is the "sneaky yellow bastards (sneaky fucker) (he who lives to get copulations)" who have mastered this evolutionary game by outwitting both the "orange bully" and "true blue" lizard compatriots. To underscore her point about the connection to contemporary Asian America, Yamashita adds, "That's right: yellows are sneaky little posers and queer to boot" (333). The language of science provides the appearance of objectivity, even as the content is deeply culturally coded. By juxtaposing lizard genetics with Asian American studies, Yamashita expresses deep skepticism of science as ever neutral or uncontaminated by cultural bias. As such, this piece shares with *Siamese Twins and Mongoloids* both affection for, and suspicion of, academic discourse, whether the discipline is ethnic studies or environmental biology.

From there, Yamashita synthesizes a variety of theories about the simple game; for example, mathematician John Forbes Nash conceptualizes rock-paper-scissors as "a zero-sum game" (337). In addition, she notes how E. coli and other harmful bacteria "also exhibit a rock-paper-scissors dynamic" (338), as do the triads of reader/writer/critic, and whites/blacks/Asian Americans in the United States. The result is a "trialectic" (as opposed to a dialectic) whereby each group has the opportunity for dominance, although "your turn may not come up for a long time (unless you're a lizard)" (344).[34] This simple triangulation is further complicated, at first comically through the Star Trek-infused version of rochambeau explained by Sheldon in the hit sitcom *The Big Bang Theory,* then more seriously when applied to the "racial pentalectics" of America governing competition among "white," "black," "brown," "red," and "yellow" communities. Yamashita then turns things again, this time back to comical, as she replaces each of those colors with musicians: Elvis (white), Michael Jackson (black), Puerto Rican pop star Ricky Martin (brown), the Native American rock group Redbone (red), and K-pop star Psy (yellow), best known for the 2012 earworm "Gangnam Style." Linking back to sexual competition, Yamashita asks, "Ladies: whom do you choose?" (348).

Yamashita's "instructions" for this performance are to assign five dancers and five musicians/instruments to enact this ritual dance of dominance and submission that is an elaborate metaphor for American anxieties about the rising economic power of China. "What will we do when those sneaky yellow bastards change the game plan?" (351).[35]

Reviews and Scholarship: *Anime Wong*

Even in the wake of the publication of *Anime Wong: Fictions of Performance,* there has been scant scholarship written about Yamashita's performance work. Sohn notes that Yamashita's theatrical works have been overlooked "because they do not function within a traditional drama setting; they often require elaborate props, staging, musical accompaniment, and costuming, and are multidisciplinary in their scope."[36] For example, a production of *GiLArex* brings major challenges to any theater company, as it includes stage directions like "*the monster rips and lifts the overpass off the freeway and carries it across the city with* MANZANAR *and* EMI *atop*" (119).[37] In one of the few scholarly analyses of the work, A. Robert Lee describes the volume as an extension of Yamashita's other works, stating it "shares the same impetus: a Japanese American theater of the satiric-baroque with props and wordplay in kind. Which is to link the collection to the novels while affording recognition of its own considerable feats of prestidigitation."[38] In many respects, Yamashita's imagination has always exceeded the capabilities of theater to realize.

Reviews of the volume in the mainstream press were positive, aptly focusing on Yamashita's originality and flamboyant theatricality. As the *Rafu Shimpo* ably described it, "Yamashita's theatrical work is fiction interpreted by the body in real time; these kinetic encounters, complete with giant foam-rubber sushi and cyborg kung fu fighters, create a space for humor, interaction, and epiphany, where Anna May Wong is transformed to Anime Wong, superstar of

CyberAsia."[39] Reviewers also recognized the collection's demands on readers, pulling them into the work as active participants. As the *Portland Review* suggested, "We as readers of *Anime Wong* can become the performers, and the plays we stage in imagination are our 'flexible rites.'"[40]

Another reason why Yamashita's performances may have been overlooked is that they have never quite found their audience, then or now. While her novels feel remarkably prescient, such as *Through the Arc of the Rainforest*'s depiction of humanity's deleterious effects on the environment long before scholars coined the term "the Anthropocene Era," her theater pieces have not aged as well as her fiction. In an interview, she admitted that "when we originally produced these performances in the 1990s, I had the feeling that they were not entirely understood, that they seemed abstract or strange or offensive to our audiences. Now they seem rather obvious and kitsch."[41] Indeed, while Yamashita's performances are provocative as political theater, they are not as effective as her longer-form fiction in terms of humanizing the very Asian American subjects she wants to release from the strictures of stereotype and caricature.

In retrospect, Yamashita's forays into theater and performance seem to work best as a rehearsal for fuller exploration in novel form. To this point, Yamashita frequently reworked ideas and even characters from her theatrical work into her novels. As she explains, "Years later, as I was writing my novel, *I Hotel,* I began to think about playwriting and documentary film scripts as forms themselves, not necessarily meant to be reproduced as film or staged as plays, but as 'fictional' forms that readers could experience simply by reading."[42] Most of the works included in *Anime Wong* were written before *Tropic of Orange* (1997), and so mark a significant transition point for her as an artist. Yamashita eventually moved away from theater once she figured out how to bend (and even break) fictional genres in order to express fully her fascinations, commitments, and untamed imagination. As she grew in confidence as a novelist, she found she could more fully express herself by writing for the audience's imagination, where nothing is impossible. And yet, it was through her theatrical experiments that Yamashita found her wondrously original, irrepressible, and outrageous creative voice.

The anger and frustration, as well as humor, that animate *Anime Wong: Fictions of Performance* become something much more focused and powerful in works like *Tropic of Orange* and *I Hotel,* which give voice to Asian American and other minority subjects seeking to define themselves in new ways that reflect their heterogeneous and multidimensional experiences and ambitions.

CHAPTER 6

Letters to Memory

I Hotel and *Letters to Memory* (2017) reflect a new phase of Yamashita's career, both formally and thematically. Formally, Yamashita has increasingly moved away from the exaggerations and absurdities of satire in favor of communal history, family history, and memoir, while maintaining her signature interest in narrative polyvocality and large-scale social canvases. Thematically, these two works emphasize how "history" is constructed personally and in relationship to others through family and community. Yamashita's most recent work, the memoir *Letters to Memory* (2017), takes these explorations further, considering her family history before and after Japanese internment, when nearly 120,000 people of Japanese descent on the West Coast—almost two-thirds of whom were American citizens—were imprisoned in camps across the desert for the duration of World War II. Ordered in 1942 by Franklin Delano Roosevelt shortly after Japan bombed Pearl Harbor, history has shown that Japanese internment was based entirely in racism and xenophobia, rather than on any evidence of disloyalty or espionage. Forced to evacuate their homes and businesses with virtually no warning, many Japanese American families lost everything.[1] In 1988 the U.S. government officially apologized for the policy, which it acknowledged was the result of "race prejudice, war hysteria and a failure of political leadership," and paid $20,000 in reparations to each survivor. In total, more than $1.6 billion were disbursed.

After the deaths of her father and his six siblings, Yamashita began to investigate the family's history as it was recorded in family photographs, artwork, letters, and "a lifetime of stuff."[2] During the process of writing, she told an interviewer, "Perhaps I should be berated for taking on such a project after they are no longer here to consult, for my tardy interest in their lives, or perhaps these things happen in their own good time, when we are ready and have the life experience to understand. Or perhaps it is my own foolish wish for the freedom of my own memories and my own way to discovery. At the same time, none of this family history belongs really to me, and like every other project, my role might be intimate and yet as stranger/observer/recorder."[3] Connecting her early work in *Brazil-Maru* and her more recent work in *I Hotel,* in *Letters to Memory* Yamashita investigates the relationship between participant and observer, individual experiences and the larger community, particularly in terms of remembering and memorializing traumatic events. *Letters to Memory* is above all a meditation on war, forgetting, remembering, and forgiveness. In *Letters to Memory,* Yamashita considers how key moments of Asian American history shaped her own family story, with a poignant sense of melancholy and contemporary urgency. The result is a narrative both personal and communal, full of archival detritus and yet inventively imagined. If her earlier works present the problems of late twentieth-century capitalism, *Letters to Memory* investigates questions of identity and the forces that shape it. Shifting between family lore and abstract ruminations on history and faith, *Letters to Memory* considers how different philosophical traditions make possible different forms of imagination, expression, and activism.

Yamashita is particularly concerned with the ways we retrospectively understand key moments of the past. *Letters to Memory* is a fragmentary exploration of her family history. In many ways *Letters to Memory* appears to be a simpler book than *I Hotel,* as it is smaller in scale and scope, focusing its aperture on the role of Japanese internment in shaping both her parents' lives and her own. But it is similarly interested in the way memory gives shape and meaning to events that are chaotic and shapeless in the moment. Although labeled a memoir, it is anything but simple or straightforward in its treatment of the subject. In some ways *Letters to Memory* is actually *more* experimental than *I Hotel,* as Yamashita makes greater use of the second person to voice a series of intellectual and familial conversations. *Letters to Memory* takes the form of imagined, one-sided correspondence with various interlocutors, inspired by and modeled on real-life colleagues and friends such as scholars James Clifford, Gildas Hamel, Ruth Hsu, Roshni Rustomji-Kerns, James Kyung-Jin Lee, and others whom she thanks in the acknowledgments. These contemporary figures are addressed via letters to iconic, historical figures from philosophy, religion, or literature who serve as muses.[4] Consequently, each interlocutor is a palimpsestic figure, who blends history and imagination. For example, Yamashita's Homer is simultaneously a college professor grading blue-book exams at a café, whose "travels and research trace the deep history of families into tribes and tribes into nations," and the author of the *Iliad,* the great epic about the Trojan War (4). Yamashita describes these interlocutors as "storytellers" who help her to weave together her particular family history and broader questions of history, narrative, trauma, and survival. The work continues Yamashita's process of formal experimentation and thematic innovation, while also representing a fitting culmination of her career.

The book is divided into five parts, each part a "letter" loosely organized around a theme in her family's life and addressed to a muse kown for writing about that theme. In the first part, "Letters to Poverty," Yamashita reads the *Iliad* as a work devoted to understanding forgiveness, inspiring her to consider her family's internment during World War II. Yamashita's father Hiroshi John Yamashita was one of seven siblings who, with their parents and three of his elder siblings' children, were imprisoned in 1942, first at the Tanforan horse-racing track near San Francisco and then in the Topaz internment camp in the Utah desert. Blending the ancient and recent past, she collapses the Trojan War and World War II, noting that "at the war's end, released to freedom, forgiveness is a radical idea, an impossibility that requires imagination" (14). Her family's experience of being treated as traitors during the war requires different forms of radical imagination to come to terms with or overcome. Yamashita's paternal grandmother Tomi refused to become a naturalized U.S. citizen as a sign of protest. John found his path through religion, as a Methodist minister; John's sister Kay became the poster child for loyal Japanese Americans among progressive Christians and to the U.S. government; John's friend Nobu Kajiwara enlisted in the Army to prove the patriotism of Japanese Americans and ultimately died for his cause. Like forgiveness, "poverty . . . can be chosen. That is its power. It occurs to me now—Kay, John, Nobu—each chose poverty" (27). With *Letters to Memory,* Yamashita continues this tradition of choosing poverty, which she frames as a kind of public service done as a means to earn one's place in the nation. Yamashita's contribution is to use her imagination as a novelist to understand the past and forgive the government for its sins against the Japanese American community.

In "Letters to Modernity," Yamashita writes to Ishi, the name given to the last Yahi Indian in California, who was the subject of several anthropological studies in the 1910s and, at the end of his life, lived in an anthropology museum at the University of California, Berkeley. This section considers the way ideas of racial or tribal allegiance serve to make some groups Other, as her Japanese American family was made outcast due to Western beliefs about Japanese "savagery." As Yamashita explains, "The very possibility of corralling a people into some kind of single tribe was born in the idea of having discovered them in the first place" (40). In other words, the discipline of anthropology, which gave birth to modern ideas about ethnic and cultural differences, also undergirded the logic that allowed for her family to be racially profiled and incarcerated. During and after the war Japanese Americans were divided into "spoilage" and "salvage," the former permanently marked as disloyal to the United States, while the latter could be rehabilitated through resettlement and relocation (40). John and his siblings were mostly salvage, scattered across the country and forced to prove their loyalty through assimilation. Yet suspicion continued. While a student at Garrett Biblical Institute (later renamed Garrett Theological Seminary) in Evanston, Illinois in 1944, John and several members of his family were prevented from renting a house due to the neighbors' anti-Japanese prejudice. Potentially even more dispiriting was the fact that distinguished faculty and community leaders did not speak up on their behalf, their espoused Christian commitments to social justice bowing to racism. John's steadfast faith, good humor, and thoroughly modern desire to "suppress the negative and sensational" are all the more remarkable in the face of white supremacy—America's own form of tribalism (58). Yamashita's letter to Ishi explores the irony that "forced internment coupled with the anthropological framing of wartime studies conspired to create the social conditions for the collective psyche of a people who . . . became *loyal* and *assimilated* and *modeled* in order to survive" (63). By the early 1960s, Japanese Americans would be touted as a "model minority"—and used to shame African American communities for their struggles—but Yamashita reminds her readers that their successful arrival into American modernity came at an incredibly steep cost. In many ways, assimilation was hardly a choice at all.

"Letters to Love" details Yamashita's parents' courtship after the war, as addressed to Vyasa, the author of the Hindu spiritual text the *Mahabarata*. At least partly modeled on Dr. Roshni Rustomji-Kerns, a writer, editor, and scholar, Yamashita's Vyasa was "born in Bombay, raised in Karachi, educated in Beirut, Durham, and Berkeley, and adopted by a second family in Oaxaca"; she can "speak Hindi, Gujarati, Urdu, English, Spanish, and read Sanskrit and Greek" (69). Most important, this Vyasa teaches Yamashita to think of community and family ties untethered to geography: "[T]he idea of a national home is antithetical to everything you believe. You would teach me that there are dreams and memories that make human creation possible, but to dream the memory of home might be the most dangerous. *It is,* you have insisted, *not always where you were born that makes you who you are*" (70). In a world of war, violence, loss, and paranoia, love is a form of resistance. Vyasa is a fitting muse, for as Yamashita acknowledges, "like the *Iliad,* the *Mahabharata* is about war, and sadly it is war and its aftermath that here haunts my family" (88).

Yamashita recounts how, in 1945 with his theology degree in hand, John moved back to California to reopen the Oakland West Tenth Japanese Methodist Church. He stocked it with cots and blankets to serve as a shelter for

Japanese returning from the camps. In 1946, in this period of post-war rebuilding, Yamashita's parents began dating. Asako Sakai was a friend of John's sister Kay. John and Asako's first date was a stereotypical (and model-minority approved) peacetime college activity: a Cal-Stanford football game. John was smitten immediately and soon asked Asako to marry him, but she deliberated for more than a year before accepting. Only much later, after John's death, did Yamashita discover why Asako hesitated. John had rather unromantically invited Asako to "*come live with me in poverty*" (84). They married in 1948. Yamashita reminds us that history is shaped not by objective "truth," but by storytellers. Yamashita's mother's silence is a reminder of stories untold, a caution against assuming that history can ever be fully known. And yet, even with such caveats, Yamashita understands John's pastoral work and his marriage to Asako as twin acts of love, designed to replace and repair communities that had been destroyed by war and injustice.

The fourth part of *Letters to Memory* is titled "Letters to Death." Directed to Ananda, disciple of the Buddha, these chapters center on loss and letting go. Yamashita details the individuals and communities destroyed by the war and considers various responses to these traumas. John lost two close friends, Nobu Kajiwara and Tyler Eitaro Nakayama. Nobu died in the army, while Tyler changed his name, abandoned his pharmacy career to become an artist, and ended the friendship. As Yamashita heartbreakingly sums up, "One friend died; another survived. Both disappeared forever" (107). John lost these friends a second time when their letters were destroyed in a basement flood. Tyler's oil painting of the West Tenth Church, which John hung above his workbench, was all that remained to commemorate what was lost. The haunting quality of Tyler's art is echoed in the stories of Japanese American artists like Miné Okubo, Chiura Obata, and Matsusaburo and Hisako Hibi—friends of the Yamashitas who used their art to protest internment and bring beauty to a world defined by ugliness.[5]

Yamashita herself is ushered into the world of loss in 1964, when her father suffered a devastating stroke. "From this moment on, I understood John to be always dying, believing that I might look away and he would be gone" (107). John eventually died in 1984. The personal and the political are intertwined, as they so often are in Yamashita's work. The pain of John's physical decline was made more poignant by the historical tragedy of the Watts riots the following year. As Yamashita laments, "What John thought, I do not know, but he stood there disabled and impotent to act or even speak. I was too young to understand the sad impossibility of John's dream of racial integration . . . Japanese and African American urban communities had been bound to each other by labor migration, racial prejudice, and housing covenants. Two decades after the war's end, the promises of racial democracy and economic well-being did not pan out for everyone" (107). In the face of such devastating losses, memory and imagination become the means of survival. Yamashita meditates to Ananda, "You think about art and music and poetry performed in other circumstances of incarceration, in death and labor camps, and point out that such creativity, using tools and any scarce materials available, is *an impulse to sustain one's humanity* and is an act of resistance. And perhaps we should add an act of witness. You remind me that while art may be spiritual practice, it is also political" (130). Yamashita's text is another brick in the bulwark against oblivion.

The final part of the book, "Letters to Laughter," is addressed to Qohelet, the author of Ecclesiastes in the Hebrew Bible and, in Yamashita's contemporary reimagining, a fellow "PK" or preacher's kid. Here Yamashita reflects on her father's theological legacy as a Methodist minister committed to social justice, which he expressed as "love and creative laughter" (150). Yamashita credits her father's obsessive sense of "calling" as "the foundation" for her own independence and artistic practice (124). Like a boomerang, she "head[ed] out in another direction which turns out anyway to be the same" as his (135). Much as John did throughout his life, Yamashita responds with humor to even the worst situations. She notes the bleak comedy of the family bringing a waffle iron and a vacuum cleaner to the internment camp, while recognizing in the absurdity a "defiant strain of rebellion and extravagance that for better or worse marks the [Yamashita] family" (139). Yamashita imagines that "someone insisted on vacuuming the empty house before finally vacating it. This idea in the face of forced evacuation seems to me so Japanese-hyphenated-American—the tacit recommendation to leave your previously occupied space cleaner than you found it" (140). In the face of dispossession, being able to tell jokes and to laugh are coping mechanisms, helping to maintain one's humanity amidst others' inhumanity. John's notes for titles of sermons to give in the camp reflect his sensibility: *Dust, Diarrhea, and Degradation; DeAmericanization in the Desert; Love's Laughter Lost; Desert Dementia; Japanese Bite the Dust*. Yamashita reads these lines and marvels, "They could be comedy routines or songs, but they are sermons" (151). Laughter, too, becomes a tool in service of spiritual education.

In 1949 John gave a sermon at his mentor Dr. Howard Thurman's interracial, interfaith Church for the Fellowship of All Peoples in San Francisco. In the sermon, entitled *The Laughter of the Human Soul*, Yamashita sees her father's philosophy spelled out: "Death was always a heartbeat away, and life, therefore, not to be taken for granted. And laughter allowed for spontaneity and exuberance and extravagance, giving balance to the tough practice of responsibility, play in the diligence of political action, freedom in intellectual pursuit"

(157). At the close of *Letters to Memory,* Yamashita wonders about her own process, "Maybe this project has been no more than an exercise in sermonizing, extracting archival letters as if scriptures, to inform or query the present" (161). In her work of memoir, much as she did in *Brazil-Maru* and *I Hotel,* Yamashita painstakingly studied the historical record in order to reassemble, or perhaps to *reanimate* it in her own writing, thereby showing its continued relevance and resonance in the present. In contemplating the impact of internment on her family's lives, Yamashita shows what Faulkner famously wrote: "The past is never dead. It's not even past."

The book as a whole considers how traumas of war and racism are internalized, repressed, and worked through in a variety of ways. The result is both destructive and creative, alienating and communal, utterly tragic and yet often comical. Much as *I Hotel* focused on the intentional community created by the Asian American movement, *Letters to Memory* interrogates conventional meanings of home and family, recognizing that home is not defined by nationality, geography, or citizenship. Likewise, family is something one is constantly making and remaking with loved ones to whom one has a biological tie, as well as those with whom one feels a sense of kinship—one's kindred spirits, without the sentimentality that phrase usually conjures. It is this restless questing for community that ties together Yamashita's letters to her intellectual companions with her study of her family history. *Letters to Memory* demonstrates Yamashita doing what her own family had to do in the wake of internment: shoring up fragments against the ruins of the modern world to create meaning amid death and dispossession.

Reviews and Scholarship: *Letters to Memory*

Reviews of *Letters to Memory* have expressed puzzlement and admiration at its patchwork approach to storytelling, which explores the painful past even as is refuses to close off meaning by providing a definitive interpretation. *Kirkus Reviews* described the work as "part research, part history, part literary criticism, part spiritual meditation, and part open wound."[6] In her *Boston Globe* review, Nina MacLaughlin described it as "a challenging, varied work, in moments deeply personal and impressionistic and in moments pulling back into a voice of epic omniscience."[7] In a familiar pattern, Yamashita's experimental form provoked polarized responses. *Publishers Weekly* lamented that "the immediacy and poignancy of the struggles of Yamashita's family members are deflated by interposed epistolary conversations with five mythic authors and pseudonymous scholars, who never take shape with the richness, complexity, urgency, or character of Yamashita's family and friends."[8] Writing for the Minneapolis *Star-Tribune,* Brigitte Frase described *Letters to Memory* as "an intriguing experiment in memoir" that emphasizes "the meta nature of Yamashita's enterprise; we are not to experience a story but are prodded to pay attention to the ways of approaching, circling it."[9]

And yet, as the *Publishers Weekly* writer begrudgingly acknowledged, the work's innovative form ultimately allows it to "make the deeper claim that there is no explanation and no possible reparation for events like slavery, internment, or the bombing of Hiroshima—only the disorienting reality they produce and the legacy of pain, distrust, and shame they leave behind."[10] In this way Yamashita puts the particularities of the Yamashita family's experiences of internment in conversation with other periods of violence throughout human history. As the reviewer for *New Pages* observed, "What sets this book apart is the addition of inventive correspondence between Yamashita and sages of old with the aim of making sense of her relatives' lives and discovering how their experiences figure into the context of history."[11] *Letters to Memory* is, like earlier work such as *Circle K Cycles,* deeply committed to understanding the patterns of human behavior across time and space.

The process of discovery animates the project, linking Yamashita's thematic interests with her formal approach. Writing for the *Kyodo News,* Justin Maki noted how "Yamashita gravitates toward lacunae in the documentary record, using the unknown—and unknowable—to fuel her philosophical queries."[12] Similarly, writing for the *Christian Science Monitor,* Terry Hong insightfully understood the work as requiring the active engagement of the reader to create meaning; her verdict was that "for all its brevity, the less-than-200 pages are dense with assumptions of cultural literacy, community insight, historical background . . . 'Letters' awaits your inquisitive participation and rewarding collaboration."[13] Yamashita has always demanded a great deal of her readers, enlisting them to help make meaning out of the past and critically understand the present. In *Brazil-Maru,* she requires her readers to participate in the process by synthesizing five narrators and making judgments about their reliability and partiality; *Through the Arc of the Rain Forest* requires a willful suspension of disbelief in order to recognize the deeper truths it reveals about global inequality; and *I Hotel* demands readers think critically about the generic forms we use to tell stories, and what they enable or preclude—whether via documentary films, comic strips, dance, drawings, poetry, or fiction. *Letters to Memory* is a fitting culmination of more than four decades of writing, incorporating all of Yamashita's intellectual fascinations and narrative tools into a single, layered work.

It is significant that none of Yamashita's letters is answered. Just as she often only had one side of the correspondence she was collecting, and so had to fill in the blanks in the historical-familial record, readers only get Yamashita's letters to her epistolary muses. *Letters to Memory* is shaped by a sense of incompleteness. Yamashita's readers are charged with imagining the response, and of carrying forth the stories of her family even as the individuals are no longer living. Fittingly for an author who spent decades writing musicals and multimedia performances, there is something quite theatrical and performative in this form, as though the entire work is a one-woman show and the readers are her audience.

Through its blend of scholarly research, family history, imagination, empathy, humor, and formal experimentation, *Letters to Memory* also can be understood as a kind of intellectual and artistic autobiography. As such, *Letters to Memory* brings a deeply personal layer to Yamashita's oeuvre, in order to explore familial and community traumas in American history, as well as the remarkable spirit of optimism and hope that created new forms of community.

Appropriately, a major thread running through *Letters to Memory* is the cyclical pattern of racial injustice, which seems to continually repeat throughout history. As in *I Hotel,* Yamashita is concerned with the opportunities taken, and those missed, to build interracial coalitions. In her own family, the connections between internment and civil rights run deep. Not only was John profoundly influenced by the racial justice work of Dr. Howard Thurman and Dr. Martin Luther King, Jr. in his clerical roles, but Yamashita sees her own youth, and later her writing career, as a continuation of this legacy. As she explains in the memoir, "My sister and I grew up boomers, our cultural nutrition a mix of soul and rock, Aretha and Baez, *I Spy* and *Captain Kangaroo*. We became part of a sansei generation who would seek to recover the history of our people's incarceration, protest the war in Vietnam, join voices and ideologies with militant paths to power and revolution" (107). In *Letters to Memory,* the injustice of internment propelled an intergenerational awareness of racial injustice and a fierce commitment to speaking out—to refusing to be the model minority, since silence brings dangers of its own. *Letters to Memory* can be read as a prequel to *I Hotel,* highlighting black-Asian connections in the decades before black power and the Asian American movement.

Throughout the memoir, Yamashita sensitively notes the moments of identification between Asian Americans and African Americans, as well as failures of empathy. Of the former, she recounts how in 1936 Howard and Sue Thurman met with Mahatma Gandhi, where they learned much about methods of peaceful protest that would transform American protest movements for decades. Thurman later helped found his Fellowship Church in the Japantown neighborhood of San Francisco, creating an interracial and interfaith ministry working for social justice. Yamashita includes the text of an anti-internment pamphlet written by pacifist Caleb Foote with input from Kay and others in the

Japanese American community, which "clearly connected Japanese American evacuation to the racism of Jim Crow, anti-Semitism, and the larger context of social justice and incarceration" (42). On Chicago's South Side in the summer of 1943, when John was in seminary and his friend Nobu was visiting from army basic training, they went to a "negro night club" where, John recalls, "they gave us the best seats in the place as cherished ethnic buddies. We were treated royally—we dined and drank and had our fill of Chicago jazz" (105). After the war, when Yamashita's maternal grandparents reopened their fish market, their first customer was a black neighbor who wanted to welcome them back.

But for all that Yamashita savors these moments of interracial communion and coalition building, she also recounts painful failures of recognition, such as her aunt Kay's "uncomfortable patronage" of a black railroad porter on a trip east while her family was interned (7). Yamashita is especially attuned to structural inequalities that put racial minorities in competition for scarce resources and opportunities. After the Japanese were evacuated from the West Coast, African Americans moved into their former neighborhoods to take jobs in the war industry. The Japanese community's losses became the black community's gain, at least for the duration of the war: "Nihonmachi became the Harlem of the West" (8). More than two decades later, John's beloved West Tenth Methodist Church in Oakland was demolished to make way for a public housing project primarily designed to serve black residents, and a new freeway that was designed to connect to a never-built bridge in San Francisco Bay. Yamashita shows how redevelopment can benefit one community at the expense of another. But more often, all minority communities are hurt by policies sacrificing organic neighborhoods in favor of social engineering. In fact, as Yamashita recounts, both the Japanese American and black communities in Oakland suffered as a result of that "disastrous urban plan of displacement and enforced segregation" (106). As she did in *I Hotel,* Yamashita gives voice not only to individuals, but to entire communities and ways of life that have repeatedly been removed, bulldozed, denied, and erased. *Letters to Memory* is a memorial to the Japanese American community and a paean to a kind of multiracial community that might yet come to fruition.

Conclusion

Yamashita began *Letters to Memory* after the deaths of the entire nisei generation of her family, culminating in her mother's death in 2015 at age 98. The project centers on events that occurred more than seventy years ago, a period that can feel as ancient and far removed as Homer's era. But the election of Donald Trump to the presidency in 2016, propelled in part by anti-immigrant and anti-diversity sentiment, made Yamashita realize the profound relevance and importance of this family story to our own time. At a reading for *Letters to Memory,* Yamashita explained that she was writing toward "some kind of reconciliation," but noted the recent rise of nativism in U.S. politics has made the fight against racism and anti-immigrant policies as necessary as ever.[14]

Indeed, Japanese internment has returned to the news lately in frightening ways. In late 2015, David Bowers, the Democratic mayor of Roanoke, Virginia justified the exclusion of Syrian refugees by invoking Japanese internment: "President Franklin D. Roosevelt felt compelled to sequester Japanese foreign nationals after the bombing of Pearl Harbor, and it appears that the threat of harm to America from ISIS now is just as real and serious as that from our enemies then."[15] Around the same period, then-candidate Donald Trump defended his proposed "Muslim ban" by citing FDR's actions after Pearl Harbor.[16] Instead of using this shameful period in American history as a warning against xenophobia and government overreach it is being used to frighten immigrant and minority communities.

In late June 2018 the injustice of the internment of Japanese Americans during World War II returned to the news when the United States Supreme Court ruled on the case *Trump v. Hawaii,* voting 5–4 to uphold the President's much-maligned travel ban. Justice Sonya Sotomayor strenuously dissented, noting that the majority used the same type of "logic" as that used in *Korematsu v. United States,* the 1944 case that upheld the internment of Japanese Americans under the guise of national security. In both cases "the exclusion order was rooted in dangerous stereotypes about, *inter alia,* a particular group's supposed inability to assimilate and desire to harm the United States."[17] The majority opinion, written by Chief Justice John Roberts, insists otherwise. He notes, "*Korematsu* has nothing to do with this case. The forcible relocation of U.S. citizens to concentration camps, solely and explicitly on the basis of race, is objectively unlawful and outside the scope of Presidential authority. But it is wholly inapt to liken that morally repugnant order to a facially neutral policy denying certain foreign nationals the privilege of admission." The Court seems to hang its ruling on the distinction between the legal rights of citizens already in the United States (in the case of *Korematsu*) and the (revocable) privileges of those seeking entry (in *Trump v. Hawaii*). Acknowledging the racism and xenophobia on which the earlier court case was based, Roberts expounds: "*Korematsu* was gravely wrong the day it was decided, has been overruled in the court of history, and—to be clear—'has no place in law under the Constitution.'" Yet for all Roberts's protestations, it is impossible not to recognize the similarities between the two cases. In the words of Erwin Chemerinsky, dean of UC Berkeley Law, "The *Korematsu* court presumed people were dangerous because they were of Japanese descent. Today, it is because they are from a particular country."[18] Regardless of the technicalities or distinctions that are being used as legal justification, the reality is that we are once again living in a historical moment when human rights have been deemed optional, a special privilege granted to a few rather than guaranteed to all.

As Michiko Kakutani, former chief book critic of the *New York Times* and author of *The Death of Truth: Notes on Falsehood in the Age of Trump*,[19] suggests in an op-ed detailing her own family's history of internment, "History is repeating itself. This time without even the pretext of war, and with added heartbreaking cruelty. Under Mr. Trump's 'zero tolerance' border enforcement policy, nearly 3,000 children were separated from their parents, and while the administration later halted these separations, it neglected to keep proper records and is now struggling to find and reunite families." Lamenting the racism and xenophobia that resulted in Kakutani's parents' and grandparents' incarceration (at the very same camps as Yamashita's family), she recalls how her mother's internment "left her with a lasting sense of the precariousness of life—the apprehension that unexpected perils could befall one at any moment."[20] This sense of instability and uncertainty created a permanent divide among Japanese Americans, between life "before" and life "after" internment. As Kakutani here suggests, and Yamashita explores in depth, these kinds of psychic wounds can never fully heal.

In this fraught contemporary political context, Yamashita's memoir serves as a necessary reminder of the humanity of those being excluded, and of the multigenerational effects such historical traumas have on families, communities, and nations. The form of Yamashita's memoir is designed to reinforce this message to readers. As she explained in an interview, *Letters to Memory* was never intended as a simple family history.

> I chose not to write a family saga, but anyone can visit the Yamashita archive [at the University of California, Santa Cruz] and reconstruct the narrative of their lives. What I wanted to explore were the gaps in their stories that connected their wartime imprisonment and dislocation to the larger story of civil rights in America. This larger story continues to be important because it is still of consequence to others—to immigrant communities, to undocumented migrant people, to Muslims and Middle Eastern people, to exiles and refugees, to all people of color, and to the very fabric of American life as we understand it to be protected by our Constitution and beliefs. What has become challenging is to face the current political climate of racism and hatred and fear that threatens hope and the long legacy of, not only my family, but of so many who have sacrificed their lives.[21]

This quotation not only crystallizes Yamashita's political and intellectual commitments in *Letters to Memory,* it also sums up Yamashita's entire oeuvre. Throughout her career Yamashita has expressed a profound sense of "responsibility" toward the real people whose lives inspire and ground her work.[22] She fills in the gaps in history, imagining the inner lives of people and places often overlooked or ignored. Without sentimentality or nostalgia, she gives her readers new ways of seeing and understanding the world around them. Her body of work examines the hopes and fears, joys and suffering, of migrants and minorities dislocated or displaced from their homes, whether by choice or necessity, for a variety of reasons: economic, intellectual, political, racial, religious, or due to war. She shows us people who are cogs in global economic systems that are cruel and that use women and men for material gain, but she also depicts individuals heroically struggling to build communities to offer succor and protection. She depicts people's pride in national identity without falling prey to jingoism or facile patriotism. Yamashita values freedom, but it is a freedom designed to create community for and among people left behind. She reminds her readers that the contemporary moment has no special access to truth, and there is no guarantee of progress or justice. We are each responsible for helping make the world more utopian, whether that be achieved in a commune in Brazil, a homeless encampment on an L.A. freeway, or an old hotel in San Francisco.

At the level of form, Yamashita models the kind of messy, beautiful, cacophonous, polyglot democracy of her dreams, where all people can speak and be heard. Her narration is playful but sincere, striving to capture individuality as well as draw attention to common experiences across people in different times and places. She explores humans' capacity for selfishness and generosity, myopia and imagination. She uses metatextual apparatuses to highlight how every story is told by a narrator with a particular axe to grind. She disrupts her own narratives by various methods, including changing perspectives, shifting genres, inserting herself in the story, or abstracting her family's experiences in order to reflect eternal experiences of love and loss and wartime. In this way, Yamashita seems to say that everyone is special and no one is unique.

In *Letters to Memory,* Yamashita reflects on her own role in the recovery project. Writing to Vyasa, she notes, "You have said that in the Vedic tradition all histories begin with the word *itihasa;* thus, it is said, and you understand this to mean that every history is a story told, weighted by the knowledge of "the teller. It is, you add, this responsibility, not only accountability, that offers truth to storytelling" (95). Yamashita is skeptical of storytelling, while acknowledging that stories are necessary for humans to give shape and meaning to their experience. She brings a questing, intellectually rigorous, humorous, and deeply humane approach to her writings about modern life in the twentieth and early twenty-first centuries. Her embrace of these contradictions and complexities makes her an apt bard for contemporary American literature. Karen Tei Yamashita is the writer we need and deserve, a Homer for the contemporary global age.

NOTES

Chapter 1: Understanding Karen Tei Yamashita

1. Cheng, Introduction to "A Twist on the Mix," *Loggernaut Reading Series,* n.p.

2. Wong, *Reading Asian American Literature: From Necessity to Extravagance.*

3. Yamashita, "Traveling Voices," 9.

4. Ibid.

5. Hong, "Interview with Karen Tei Yamashita," n.p.

6. Yamashita, Kay, transcript of an oral history conducted in 1991, in *Yamashita Family Archives,* UC Santa Cruz Library, University of California, Santa Cruz, n.p.

7. From a national security standpoint, it would have been more logical for the government to demand closer surveillance of Japanese Americans in Hawai'i than on the mainland, since Honolulu was the starting point for the war and is geographically closer to Japan. And indeed, the U.S. government put Hawai'i under martial law for the duration of the war. But the 158,000 Japanese Americans in Hawai'i, constituting more than one third of the territory's total population, did not face mass incarceration the way Japanese Americans on the mainland did. Instead, only 2,000 *kibei* (American-born Japanese who were educated in Japan) were interned, and they were mostly sent to camps on the mainland. This suggests that internment was driven by paranoia and xenophobia, not by actual military intelligence or evidence. In fact, not one person of Japanese descent living in the United States was ever convicted of any serious crime of espionage or sabotage during the war.

8. Yun, "Interview with Karen Tei Yamashita," 206.

9. Jacobson, "Alumni Profile: Karen Tei Yamashita ('73)," n.p.

10. Shan, "Interview with Karen Tei Yamashita," 124.

11. Yamashita, *Circle K Cycles,* 12.

12. Yamashita, "Writing and Memory," 217.

13. Cheng, "A Twist on the Mix," *Loggernaut Reading Series,* n.p.

14. Shan, "Interview with Karen Tei Yamashita," 130.

15. Johnston, "Karen Tei Yamashita Interview," n.p.

16. Yamashita, "Reimagining Traveling Bodies," 166.

17. Hong, "Interview with Karen Tei Yamashita," n.p.

18. Yamashita, "Reimagining Traveling Bodies," 169.

19. Hong, "Interview with Karen Tei Yamashita," n.p.

20. Yamashita, "Traveling Voices," 10.

21. This play is sometimes rendered as *O-men.*

22. Imafuku, "The Latitude of the Fiction Writer: A Dialogue with Karen Tei Yamashita," n.p.

23. Shan, "Interview with Karen Tei Yamashita," 132.
24. Yun, "Interview with Karen Tei Yamashita," 208.
25. Campbell, review of *Through the Arc of the Rain Forest.*
26. *Kirkus,* review of *Brazil-Maru.*
27. Shan, "Interview with Karen Tei Yamashita," 135.
28. Morales, review of *Tropic of Orange.*
29. Magosaki, *Tricksters & Cosmopolitans,* 11.
30. Mahoney, review of *Circle K Cycles.*
31. Shan, "Interview with Karen Tei Yamashita," 141–142.
32. Yamashita, "The Santa Cruz of Tofu," n.p.
33. Quoted in Palumbo-Liu, "Embedded Lives," 17.
34. "United States Artists," http://www.unitedstatesartists.org/about/ (accessed June 8, 2018).
35. MacLaughlin, "Kaleidoscopic Look at Japanese Internment Camps." Review of *Letters to Memory,* n.p.
36. Ling, "Forging a North-South Perspective," 1.
37. Ibid.
38. Glixman, "Interview with Karen Tei Yamashita," n.p.
39. Yamashita, "Writing and Memory," 219.
40. Imafuku, "The Latitude of the Fiction Writer," n.p.
41. Ibid.
42. Williams, "Blending and Bending the Borders," F15.
43. Yun, "Interview with Karen Tei Yamashita," 209.
44. Shan, "Interview with Karen Tei Yamashita," 138.
45. Porte, "Interview with Author Karen Tei Yamashita," n.p.
46. Chrisman and Sexton, "A Boom Interview: Karen Tei Yamashita," 24.
47. Yun, "Interview with Karen Tei Yamashita," 204.
48. Chrisman and Sexton, "A Boom Interview: Karen Tei Yamashita," 20.

Chapter 2: *Brazil-Maru, Through the Arc of the Rain Forest,* and *Circle K Cycles*

1. Shan, "Interview with Karen Tei Yamashita," 134.
2. Murashige, "Interview with Karen Tei Yamashita," 323.
3. Gier and Tejeda, "An Interview with Karen Tei Yamashita," n.p.
4. Yamashita, "Writing and Memory," 218.
5. Yamashita, "Traveling Voices," 9.
6. Cheng, "A Twist on the Mix," *Loggernaut Reading Series,* n.p.
7. Yamashita, *Brazil-Maru,* 124. All further references to this work are cited in the text.
8. In "Epilogue (2): Tamahori," a metatextual postscript to *Brazil-Maru* that was published later, a character describes the colony as "like a museum. Even the people." Yamashita, *Writing and Memory,* 225.
9. Sugano, "Karen Tei Yamashita," 406.
10. Thoma, "Traveling the Distances of Karen Tei Yamashita's Fiction: A Review Essay on Yamashita Scholarship and Transnational Studies, 12; Song, *The Children of 1965: On Writing, and Not Writing, as an Asian American,* 182n7.
11. See Terazawa, "'Shifting the Pattern of History'" and "Collective Memory and Camera Images in Karen Tei Yamashita's *Brazil-Maru.*"
12. Hsu, review of *Brazil-Maru, 189.*

13. Chuh, "Of Hemispheres and Other Spheres: Navigating Karen Tei Yamashita's Literary World," 625.

14. Birns, "An Incomplete Journey: Settlement and Power in *Brazil-Maru,*" 95.

15. Ling, "Forging a North-South Perspective," 6.

16. Hong, "Interview with Karen Tei Yamashita," n.p.

17. Yamashita, "Call Me Ishimaru," 64. In an interview, Yamashita claimed that Kazumasa was also based on a family friend who moved to Brazil after World War II. Murashige, "Interview with Karen Tei Yamashita," 326.

18. Yamashita described Tweep as "a kind of nerdy modern-day Ahab" (ibid., 65).

19. Yamashita, *Through the Arc of the Rain Forest,* 211. All further references to this work are cited in the text.

20. Rody, "Impossible Voices: Ethnic Postmodern Narration in Toni Morrison's *Jazz* and Karen Tei Yamashita's *Through the Arc of the Rain Forest,*" 629.

21. Campbell, review of *Through the Arc of the Rain Forest.*

22. Harris, "The Narrative Arts," n.p.

23. Heise, "Local Rock and Global Plastic: World Ecology and the Experience of Place," 132.

24. Ling, *Across Meridians,* 105.

25. Bahng, "Extrapolating Transnational Arcs, Excavating Imperial Legacies: The Speculative Acts of Karen Tei Yamashita's *Through the Arc of the Rain Forest,*" 124.

26. Murashige, "Interview with Karen Tei Yamashita," 328.

27. Wallace, "'A Bizarre Ecology': The Nature of Denatured Nature," 145.

28. Ibid., 146.

29. Simal et al., "Of a Magical Nature," 194.

30. Cheung, "Re-Viewing Asian American Literary Studies," 19.

31. Lee, "Asian American Cultural Production in Asia-Pacific Perspective," 241.

32. Ibid., 239.

33. Hong, "Interview with Karen Tei Yamashita," n.p.

34. Watson, "Yamashita Honored by UCSC Distinguished Teaching Award," B-2.

35. Brada-Williams, "Twenty Years after *Through the Arc of the Rain Forest:* An Interview with Karen Tei Yamashita," 1.

36. In *Circle K Cycles,* Yamashita gives the following definition of "Nikkei": "of Japanese ancestry or lineage; belonging to the Japanese tribe; however, some dictionaries translate this word to mean Japanese emigrant, or even Japanese American." Yamashita, *Circle K Cycles,* 10.

37. Mahoney, review of *Circle K Cycles.*

38. Picone, review of *Circle K Cycles.*

39. *Publisher's Weekly,* review of *Circle K Cycles.*

40. Ling, *Across Meridians,* 73.

41. Ragain, "(Re)Production Cycles: Labor and National Identity in *Circle K Cycles,*" 140.

42. Chuh, "Of Hemispheres and Other Spheres," 622.

Chapter 3: *Tropic of Orange*

1. Murashige, "Interview with Karen Tei Yamashita," 340.

2. Glixman, "Interview with Karen Tei Yamashita," n.p.

3. Ibid.

4. Yamashita, "The Orange," 12.

5. Ibid.
6. Arias, "NAFTA: The Good, the Bad, and the Ugly," 30.
7. Ibid.
8. Karpilow et al., "NAFTA: 20 Years of Costs to Communities and the Environment," 1–20.
9. McAuliff, "NAFTA Report Warns of Trade Deal Environmental Disasters," n.p.
10. Gier and Tejeda, "An Interview with Karen Tei Yamashita," n.p.
11. Shan, "Interview with Karen Tei Yamashita," 135.
12. Ibid.
13. Ibid.
14. Murashige, "Interview with Karen Tei Yamashita," 339.
15. Yamashita, *Tropic of Orange,* 15. All further references to this work are cited within the text. The character of Bobby was inspired by someone whom Yamashita worked with at a public television station. (As discussed in the first chapter, Yamashita worked at a public television station for thirteen years.)
16. Murashige, "Interview with Karen Tei Yamashita," 340.
17. Gier and Tejeda, "An Interview with Karen Tei Yamashita," n.p.
18. Morales, review of *Tropic of Orange.*
19. Rauch, "Fruit Salad." Review of *Tropic of Orange,* 28.
20. Kaye, review of *Tropic of Orange.*
21. Vint, "Orange County: Global Networks in *Tropic of Orange,*" 405.
22. Wallace, "Tropics of Globalization: Reading the New North America," 155.
23. Mermann-Jozwiak, "Yamashita's Post-National Spaces," 2.
24. Entin, "Globalization, Migration, and Contemporary Working-Class Literature," 390.
25. Adams, "The Ends of America, the Ends of Postmodernism," 248.
26. Hsu, "The Cartography of Justice and Truthful Refraction Found in Karen Tei Yamashita's *Tropic of Orange,*" 95.
27. Magosaki, *Tricksters & Cosmopolitans,* 88.
28. Lowe, Lisa, *Immigrant Acts,* 60.
29. Crawford, "From Desert Dust to City Soot," 87.
30. Rody, "The Transnational Imagination," 132.
31. Chae, *Politicizing Asian American Literature,* 93.
32. Melamed, *Represent and Destroy,* 93.
33. Santa Ana, *Racial Feelings,* 225.
34. Lee, "We Are Not the World," 502.

Chapter 4: *I Hotel*

1. Chuh, "Karen Tei Yamashita Interviewed," 104.
2. Shavers, "Recuperating History: An Interview with Karen Tei Yamashita," n.p.
3. Porte, "Interview with Author Karen Tei Yamashita," n.p.
4. Yamashita, "I Hotel: An Introduction for Amerasia," 23.
5. Imafuku, "The Latitude of the Fiction Writer," n.p.
6. Yamashita again reworked the initial version of "Siamese Twins and Mongoloids" into a piece by the same name that was published in *Anime Wong* (2014), a collection of performance works edited by Asian American studies scholar Stephen Hong Sohn.
7. Chuh, "Karen Tei Yamashita Interviewed," 100.
8. Chiapella, "A Talk with Karen Tei Yamashita," n.p.

9. Shavers, "Recuperating History," n.p.
10. Zisler, review of *I Hotel,* 78.
11. Dong, "Third World Liberation Comes to San Francisco State and UC Berkeley," 95.
12. "Investors Shaking Threads in Urban Spider Web," 1.
13. In naming these characters "Chang" and "Eng," Yamashita deliberately and comically echoes the conjoined Bunker twins from Thailand who were famous in the nineteenth century, first as sideshow displays and later as genteel husbands, fathers, and farmers. For more on these fascinating historical figures, see Cynthia Wu, *Chang and Eng Reconnected: The Original Siamese Twins in American Culture* (Philadelphia: Temple University Press, 2012).
14. Palumbo-Liu, "Embedded Lives," 17.
15. Quoted in Palumbo-Liu, "Embedded Lives," 17.
16. Hua, Review of *I Hotel,* n.p.
17. Cheuse, Review of *I Hotel,* n.p.
18. Shavers, "Recuperating History," n.p.
19. Ragain, "A Revolutionary Romance," 139.
20. Eng, "Queer Genealogies of (Be)Longing," 353.
21. This also serves to complicate Ralph Ellison's infamous distinction between literary "relatives" who share one's racial/cultural context and the artistic "ancestors" one might claim based on aesthetic criteria.
22. Yu, "Capturing the Spirit," 68.
23. Lee, "House of Memory," 145–146.
24. Jin, "Inconspicuous Magic," 465.
25. Wong, "Dwelling over China," 723.

Chapter 5: *Anime Wong*

1. Several of the early works are available in the Special Collections and University Archives of the University of Massachusetts Amherst, in the Roberta Uno Asian American Women Playwrights Script Collection 1924–2002.
2. Lee, "Interview: Karen Tei Yamashita," n.p.
3. Morley and Robins, "Techno-Orientalism."
4. Ray, "Possibilities Remain Vibrant within Yamashita's *Anime Wong,*" 11.
5. Yamashita herself requested that her earliest play *Omen: An American Kabuki* (sometimes reproduced as *O-Men,* 1978) not be published. *Hiroshima Tropical* (1984), an unfinished work in progress, and the unproduced play version of *Asaka-no-Miya* (1984) were set in the Japanese Brazilian community in Brazil, and so lacked the U.S.-centric transnational consciousness common to the rest of the volume. *Rock Candy* (1987), a musical about an all-women rock band created with Vicki Abe, was excluded because it had never been completed or staged, nor did it deal with Asian American themes.
6. Yamashita and Burns, "Anime Wong: Mobilizing (techno)Orientalism," 181.
7. Song, "*Anime Wong*: A Critical Afterword," 364.
8. Yamashita and Burns, "Anime Wong: Mobilizing (techno)Orientalism," 176.
9. Ibid., 185.
10. Sohn, "*Anime Wong*: A Critical Afterword," 365.
11. Lee, "Shift of Scene," 155–156.
12. Sohn, "*Anime Wong*: A Critical Afterword, 366.
13. Yamashita plays with the idea of "pickling" the past in *Brazil-Maru*'s Japanese colony in Brazil.

14. Murashige, "Interview with Karen Tei Yamashita," 340.

15. The idea of L.A. being transformed by damage to the highway system is further imagined in *Tropic of Orange,* when the freeway becomes home to an alternative community. Another idea from the musical that Yamashita reworks in *Tropic of Orange* is the metaphor of L.A. as "the Big Orange," as the character version of (real-life) Mayor Jane Olvera refers to the city as "mi naranja dulce" (121).

16. Yamashita, *Anime Wong,* 51.

17. Ibid.

18. Yamashita and Burns, "Anime Wong: Mobilizing (techno)Orientalism," 186.

19. Baird, "Butoh: Dance of Darkness and Light," 321.

20. Ibid.

21. White people's fascination with and fantasies about Japanese culture are echoed in *Tropic of Orange,* when Emi highlights the condescension and ignorance of the white woman who claims to love sushi and respect Japanese culture but wears chopsticks in her hair.

22. Segal, "Performance Art Review: 'Hannah Kusoh,'" calendar part 6, p.4.

23. Curtis, "Performance Art Review: Five Uneven Pieces," F14.

24. In the production at the Taper, Too, there were six actors, all of whom were Asian American, with the "white" roles played by actors in whiteface makeup. I do not know precisely how the roles were divided up in that production, or if alterations were made to the text.

25. These are the final words of the aria, which Yamashita translates in her epigraph as "Keep your fears; I, with secure faith, wait for him" (61).

26. She would return to this structure in extended and multi-genre format in *I Hotel.*

27. Kagaya and Hiroki, "Noh and Muromachi Culture," 24.

28. Yamashita and Burns, "Anime Wong: Mobilizing (techno)Orientalism," 178.

29. Sohn, "Introduction: Alien/Asian: Imagining the Racialized Future," 6.

30. Sohn, "*Anime Wong*: A Critical Afterword," 380.

31. The character is named after Yamashita's colleague and friend, Asian American theater scholar and dramaturge Lucy Mae San Pablo Burns.

32. Mike Kato appears to be the author of the parodied work of ethnic studies scholarship that Yamashita developed in the 1990s, titled "Siamese Twins and Mongoloids: Cultural Appropriation and the Deconstruction of Stereotype Via the Absurdity of Humor." See previous chapter, footnotes 3–6, for more on this work.

33. Sylvia Shin Huey Chong describes the vertiginous experience for Asian Americans in the wake of the Virginia Tech massacre of realizing "an act of Asian violence that instigates the racializing gaze, awakening Asian Americans from their slumber of seeming racial invisibility" (Chong, "'Look, an Asian!'," 32).

34. Yamashita's use of trialectics here echoes and builds upon her exploration of this idea in *Through the Arc of the Rain Forest.*

35. Sohn, "*Anime Wong*: A Critical Afterword," 364.

36. Ibid., 358.

37. In its production in Seattle, puppeteers manipulated dolls on a miniature version of Los Angeles.

38. Lee, "Shift of Scene," 155.

39. *Rafu Shimpo,* review of *Anime Wong,* n.p.

40. *Portland Review,* review of *Anime Wong,* n.p.

41. Ibid.

42. Yamashita and Burns, "Anime Wong: Mobilizing (techno)Orientalism," 180.

Chapter 6: *Letters to Memory*

1. Japanese American families are estimated to have lost more than a billion dollars in wealth and property.

2. Yamashita, *Letters to Memory,* x. All further references to this work are cited within the text.

3. Yun, "Interview with Karen Tei Yamashita," 206–207.

4. *Letters to Memory* was initially titled *Scintillations,* in reference to her father John's demand for "scintillating" conversation as recompense for the elaborate meals he cooked for family and friends.

5. Miné Okubo painted alongside Diego Rivera for the Works Progress Administration.

6. *Kirkus Reviews,* review of *Letters to Memory,* n.p.

7. MacLaughlin, "Kaleidoscopic Look at Japanese Internment Camps," n.p.

8. *Publishers Weekly,* review of *Letters to Memory,* n.p.

9. Frase, review of *Letters to Memory,* n.p.

10. *Publishers Weekly,* review of *Letters to Memory,* n.p.

11. *New Pages,* review of *Letters to Memory,* n.p.

12. Maki, "Japanese American Authors Expand Frame in Works on WWII Internee Kin," n.p.

13. Hong, review of *Letters to Memory,* n.p.

14. Maki, "Japanese American Authors Expand Frame in Works on WWII Internee Kin," n.p.

15. Weiner, "Roanoke Mayor David Bowers: Reject Refugees Like US Interned Japanese," n.p.

16. Keneally, "Donald Trump Cites These FDR Policies to Defend Muslim Ban," n.p.

17. Sotomayor, dissenting opinion, *Trump v. Hawaii,* 26–27.

18. Paul and Selk, "How the Supreme Court Struck Down a WWII-Era Travesty," n.p.

19. Kakutani, *The Death of Truth: Notes on Falsehood in the Age of Trump* (New York: Tim Duggan Books, 2018).

20. Kakutani, "I Know What Incarceration Does to Families: It Happened to Mine," n.p.

21. Jacobson, "Alumni Profile," n.p.

22. Johnston, "Karen Tei Yamashita Interview," n.p.

SELECTED BIBLIOGRAPHY

Works by Karen Tei Yamashita

NOVELS AND FULL-LENGTH WORKS

Through the Arc of the Rain Forest. Minneapolis: Coffeehouse Press, 1990.

Brazil-Maru. Minneapolis: Coffeehouse Press, 1992.

Tropic of Orange. Minneapolis: Coffeehouse Press, 1997.

Circle K Cycles. Minneapolis: Coffeehouse Press, 2001.

I Hotel. Minneapolis: Coffeehouse Press, 2010.

Anime Wong: Fictions of Performance. Minneapolis: Coffeehouse Press, 2014.

Letters to Memory. Minneapolis: Coffeehouse Press, 2017.

SELECTED SHORT FICTION, ESSAYS, AND PERFORMANCE PIECES

"The Bath." *Amerasia Journal* 3.1 (1975): 137–52. Reprinted in *The Third Woman: Minority Women Writers of the United States*, 505–19. Ed. Dexter Fisher. New York: Houghton Mifflin, 1980.

"Tucano." *Rafu Shimpo* (December 20, 1975): holiday ed: 11, 35.

Omen: An American Kabuki. 1978. Produced by East West Players in Los Angeles. Available through New World Theater, University of Massachusetts Amherst.

"Asaka-no-Miya." *Rafu Shimpo* (December 20, 1979): holiday ed.: 8–10, 16–17, 20.

"Obasan." In *Calafia: The California Poetry*. Ed. Ishmael Reed. Berkeley: Yardbird Books, 1979. 375–77.

"Maceio Maceio." *Ayumi: A Japanese American Anthology*. Ed. Janice Mirikitani. San Francisco: Japanese American Anthology Committee, 1980.

Hiroshima Tropical. 1984. Produced as a work in progress by East West Players in Los Angeles. Available through New World Theater, University of Massachusetts Amherst.

"The Dentist and the Dental Hygienist." *Asiam* 2 (1987): 66–70. Reprinted in *Hermes* 55 (1995): 125–35.

Hannah Kusoh: An American Butoh. 1989. Reprinted in *Anime Wong: Fictions of Performance*, 21–52. Minneapolis: Coffeehouse Press, 2014.

"The Japanese Brazilians." *Rafu Shimpo* (December 16, 1989): A4–A8, B27–B31.

"The Orange." *Los Angeles Times Magazine*, June 30, 1991: 12–13, 36. Reprinted in *Chicago Review* 39.3–4 (1993): 12–16 and *Hermes* 55 (1995): 121–25.

"Madama B." *International Examiner*, May 5–18, 1993, 17–19. Reprinted in *Anime Wong: Fictions of Performance*, 59–72. Minneapolis: Coffeehouse Press, 2014.

"Virtual Reality vs. Magic Reality." *Subaru* 8 (August 1995): 180–84.

"The Last Secretary." *2000andWhat?: Stories about the Turn of the Millennium*. Ed. David Gilbert and Karl Roeseler. San Francisco: Trip Street Press, 1996. 191–201.

"Purely Japanese." *Café Creole*. 1997. http://www.cafecreole.net/travelogue/karen-e.html.

"Siamese Twins and Mongoloids: Cultural Appropriation and the Deconstruction of Stereotype via the Absurdity of Humor." *DisOrient* 4 (1997): 60–68. Reprinted in *Anime Wong: Fictions of Performance* as "Siamese Twins and Mongoloids: Three Abstractions on Asian America," 261–88. Minneapolis: Coffeehouse Press, 2014.

"The Santa Cruz of Tofu." *Café Creole*. September 1998. http://www.cafecreole.net/travelogue/karen/circleK2.html#september1998.

"A Gaveta da Celia." *Café Creole*. October 1998. http://www.cafecreole.net/travelogue/karen/circleK2.html#october1998.

"Y2CircleK." *Café Creole*. May 1999. http://www.cafecreole.net/travelogue/karen/circleK2.html#may1999.

"Traveling Voices." *Café Creole*. June 2000. http://www.cafecreole.net/travelogue/karen/circleK2.html#june2000. Reprinted in *Comparative Literature Studies* 45.1 (2008): 4–11.

"Bloodtype."*Café Creole*. 9 August, 2004. http://www.cafecreole.net/travessia/bloodtype.html.

"I Hotel: An Introduction for *Amerasia*," *Amerasia Journal* 32.2 (2006): 23–46.

"Borges & I." *Massachusetts Review* 53.2 (2012): 209–14.

"Writing and Memory: Images of the Japanese Diaspora in Brazil. *Orientalism and Identity in Latin America: Fashioning Self and Other from the (Post)Colonial Margin*. Ed. Erik Camayd-Freixas. Tucson: University of Arizona Press, 2013. 217–29.

"I, Kitty." *Ploughshares* 40.2, 3 (2014): 183–87.

"Call Me Ishimaru." *Leviathan* 18.1 (2016): 64–75.

"Reimagining Traveling Bodies: Bridging the Future/Past." In *Karen Tei Yamashita: Fictions of Magic and Memory*, edited by A. Robert Lee, 163–76. Honolulu: University of Hawai'i Press, 2018.

Yamashita, Karen Tei. "Literature as Community: *The Turtle, Imagination, & The Journey Home*." *The Massachusetts Review*, vol. 59 no. 4, 2018, pp. 597–611. *Project Muse*, doi: 10.1353/mar.2018.0090

INTERVIEWS WITH KAREN TEI YAMASHITA

Brada-Williams, Noelle. "Twenty Years after *Through the Arc of the Rain Forest:* An Interview with Karen Tei Yamashita." *Asian American Literature: Discourse & Pedagogies* 1.1 (2010): 1–5. ezproxy.bgsu.edu:8080/login?url=http://search.ebscohost.com/login.aspx?direct=true&db=lkh&AN=70093149&site=ehost-live&scope=site (accessed November 16, 2017).

Cheng, Wendy. "Karen Tei Yamashita: A Twist on the Mix." *Loggernaut Reading Series*. http://www.loggernaut.org/interviews/karenteiyamashita/kty4.php (accessed March 22, 2018).

Chiapella, Julia. "A Talk with Karen Tei Yamashita." *phren-z: An Online Literary Magazine for Santa Cruz County* 1.1 (Winter 2012). http://phren-z.org/Winter2012/juliachiapella.html (accessed July 21, 2018).

Chrisman, Jonathan, and Jason S. Sexton. "A Boom Interview: Karen Tei Yamashita."

Boom: A Journal of California, 6.3 (Fall 2016): 18–24. doi: 10.1525/boom.2016.6.3.18 (accessed July 21, 2018).

Chuh, Kandice. "Karen Tei Yamashita Interviewed by Kandice Chuh." *Asian American Literary Review* 1.1 (Spring 2010): 97–107. ezproxy.bgsu.edu:8080/login?url =http://search.ebscohost.com/login.aspx?direct=true&db=lkh&AN=84013386&site =ehost-live&scope=site (accessed July 21, 2018).

Gier, Jean Vengua and Carla Alicia Tejeda. "An Interview with Karen Tei Yamashita." *Jouvert: A Journal of Postcolonial Studies.* University of California, Berkeley, 1998. https://legacy.chass.ncsu.edu/jouvert/v2i2/YAMASHI.htm (accessed July 21, 2018).

Glixman, Elizabeth P. "An Interview with Karen Tei Yamashita." *Eclectica Magazine.* Oct/Nov 2007. http://www.eclectica.org/v11n4/glixman_yamashita.html (accessed October 25, 2017).

Hong, Terry. "An Interview with Karen Tei Yamashita." *Bookslut.* July 2010. http://www .bookslut.com/features/2010_07_016303.php (accessed February 9, 2017).

Imafuku, Ryuta. "The Latitude of the Fiction Writer: A Dialogue with Karen Tei Yamashita." *Cafecreole.net.* http://www.cafecreole.net/archipelago/Karen_Dialogue.html (accessed July 21, 2018).

Johnston, Bret Anthony. "Karen Tei Yamashita Interview." *National Book Foundation.* 2010. http://www.nationalbook.org/nba2010_f_yamashita_interv.html#.W1NM2NJ KjIU (accessed May 31, 2018).

Lee, Karen An-hwei. "Interview: Karen Tei Yamashita." *Your Impossible Voice.* May 5, 2014. http://www.yourimpossiblevoice.com/karen-hwei-lee-reads/ (accessed October 25, 2017).

Murashige, Michael S. "Interview with Karen Tei Yamashita." In *Words Matter: Conversations with Asian American Writers,* edited by King-Kok Cheung, 321–42. Honolulu: University of Hawai'i Press, 2000.

Porte, Clint. "Interview with Author Karen Tei Yamashita by Clint Porte (Tufts University)." *Reader's Guide to I Hotel by Students in Grace Talusan's Class English 2 Asian American Experience,* edited by Grace Talusan. March 10, 2011. http://ihotelguide .blogspot.com/p/interview-with-author-karen-tei.html (accessed May 30, 2018).

Shan, Te-hsing. "Interview with Karen Tei Yamashita." *Amerasia Journal* 32.3 (2006): 123–42. https://doi-org.ezproxy.bgsu.edu:9443/10.17953/amer.32.3.c0g306560885r28 (accessed July 21, 2018).

Shavers, Rone. "Recuperating History: An Interview with Karen Tei Yamashita." *Fiction Writers Review.* August 14, 2013. https://fictionwritersreview.com/tag/karen-tei -yamashita/k (accessed May 30, 2018).

Watson, Chris. "Yamashita Honored by UCSC Distinguished Teacher Award." *Santa Cruz Sentinel,* June 3, 2001: B-2.

Yamashita, Karen Tei and Lucy Mae San Pablo Burns. "Anime Wong: Mobilizing (techno)Orientalism—Artistic Keynote and Conversation." *Journal of Contemporary Drama in English,* 5.1 (2017): 173–88. doi: 10.1515/jcde-2017–013 (accessed May 22, 2018).

Yun, Lisa. "Signifying 'Asian' and Afro-Cultural Poetics: A Conversation with William Luis, Albert Chong, Karen Tei Yamashita, and Alejandro Campos García." *Afro-Hispanic Review,* 27.1 (Spring 2008): 183–217. https://www-jstor-org.ezproxy.bgsu.edu:9443/ stable/23055231 (accessed July 13, 2018).

Secondary Sources

REVIEWS

Campbell, John R. B. Review of *Through the Arc of the Rain Forest,* by Karen Tei Yamashita. *New York Times,* March 10, 1991: BR16. https://search.proquest.com/docview/108828046?accountid=26417 (accessed October 24, 2017).

Cheuse, Alan. Review of *I Hotel,* by Karen Tei Yamashita. *Chicago Tribune*, October 18, 2010. http://www.chicagotribune.com/lifestyles/books/chi-books-review-i-hotel-yamashita-story.html (accessed October 25, 2017).

Curtis, Cathy. "Performance Art Review: Five Uneven Pieces in 'the 13th Hour' at the Taper Too." *Los Angeles Times,* June 30, 1990: F14. https://search.proquest.com/docview/281146390?accountid=26417 (accessed July 21, 2018).

Frase, Brigitte. Review of *Letters to Memory,* by Karen Tei Yamashita. *Minneapolis Star-Tribune.* September 1, 2017. http://www.startribune.com/review-letters-to-memory-by-karen-tei-yamashita/442405623/ (accessed June 4, 2018).

Harris, Michael. "The Narrative Arts: Through the Arc of the Rain Forest." Review of *Through the Arc of the Rain Forest,* by Karen Tei Yamashita. *Los Angeles Times,* September 9, 1990: n.p. https://search.proquest.com/docview/281258912?accountid=26417 (accessed October 25, 2017).

Hong, Terry A. "Midwestern Mu-Vement: Terry Hong Checks Out the Most Innovative Outpost in Asian American Theater, Theater Mu in Minneapolis." *A.Magazine*, November, 30 1996: 92. https://search.proquest.com/docview/200178615?accountid=26417 (accessed June 4, 2018).

Hong, Terry. "'Letters to Memory' Tells the Story of Author Karen Tei Yamashita's World War II Internment." *The Christian Science Monitor,* September 13, 2017. https://search.proquest.com/docview/1938162108?accountid=26417 (accessed May 31, 2018).

Hsu, Ruth. Review of *Brazil-Maru. Manoa* 5.2 (1993): 188–90. https://www-jstor-org.ezproxy.bgsu.edu:9443/stable/4228955 (accessed May 22, 2018).

Hua, Vanessa. Review of *I Hotel,* by Karen Tei Yamashita. *SF Gate,* May 16, 2010: n.p. https://www.sfgate.com/books/article/I-Hotel-by-Karen-Tei-Yamashita-3264222.php (accessed October 25, 2017).

"Karen Yamashita's Latest: 'Anime Wong.'" *Rafu Shimpo: Los Angeles Japanese Daily News,* March 5, 2014. http://www.rafu.com/2014/03/karen-yamashitas-latest-anime-wong/ (accessed November 16, 2017).

Kaye, Janet. Review of *Tropic of Orange,* by Karen Tei Yamashita. *New York Times,* January 4, 1998: BR16. https://archive.nytimes.com/www.nytimes.com/books/98/01/04/bib/980104.rv143527.html (accessed October 24, 2017).

Ling, Jinqi. Review of *I Hotel. Amerasia Journal* 36.3 (2010): 149. https://doi-org.ezproxy.bgsu.edu:9443/10.17953/amer.36.3.f26v45013uv8226w (accessed July 21, 2018).

MacLaughlin, Nina. "Kaleidoscopic Look at Japanese Internment Camps." Review of *Letters to Memory. Boston Globe,* September 8, 2017. https://www.bostonglobe.com/arts/books/2017/09/07/kaleidoscopic-look-japanese-internment-camps/SScNSJwdxdhytwifH8qUQI/story.html (accessed June 4, 2018).

Mahoney, Leo J. Review of *Circle K Cycles,* by Karen Tei Yamashita. *Multicultural Review* 10.4 (2001): 82–83.ezproxy.bgsu.edu:8080/login?url=http://search.ebscohost.com/login.aspx?direct=true&db=ehh&AN=15518852&site=ehost-live&scope=site (accessed November 16, 2017).

Maki, Justin. "Japanese American Authors Expand Frame in Works on WWII Internee Kin." *Kyodo News,* March 26, 2018. https://english.kyodonews.net/news/2018/03/40b272e9dda5-feature-japanese-american-authors-expand-frame-in-works-on-wwii-internee-kin.html (accessed June 4, 2018).

McNamee, Gregory. Review of *I Hotel. Kirkus Reviews,* November 15, 2010: 179. *EBSCOhost.* ezproxy.bgsu.edu:8080/login?url=http://search.ebscohost.com/login.aspx?direct=true&db=a9h&AN=55823931&site=ehost-live&scope=site (accessed May 31, 2018).

Morales, Ed. Review of *Tropic of Orange,* by Karen Tei Yamashita. *Village Voice,* September 30, 1997: 61. https://search.proquest.com/docview/232196413?accountid=26417 (accessed November 16, 2017).

Picone, Jason. Review of *Circle K Cycles,* by Karen Tei Yamashita. *Review of Contemporary Fiction* 22.1 (2002): 135. ezproxy.bgsu.edu:8080/login?url=http://search.ebscohost.com/login.aspx?direct=true&db=a9h&AN=6236127&site=ehost-live&scope=site (accessed November 16, 2017).

Rauch, Molly. "Fruit Salad." Review of *Tropic of Orange,* by Karen Tei Yamashita." *Nation,* March 2, 1998: 28–30. ezproxy.bgsu.edu:8080/login?url=http://search.ebscohost.com/login.aspx?direct=true&db=a9h&AN=253401&site=ehost-live&scope=site (accessed November 16, 2017).

Ray, Roxanne. "Possibilities Remain Vibrant within Yamashita's *Anime Wong.*" Seattle *International Examiner,* July 1, 2015: 11. https://search.proquest.com/docview/1712301101?accountid=26417 (accessed November 16, 2017).

Review of *Anime Wong,* by Karen Tei Yamashita. *Portland Book Review,* September 24, 2014. http://portlandbookreview.com/2014/09/anime-wong-fictions-of-performance-by-karen-tei-yamashita/ (accessed October 25, 2017).

Review of *Brazil-Maru,* by Karen Tei Yamashita. *Kirkus Reviews,* July 1, 1992. https://advance-lexis-com.ezproxy.bgsu.edu:9443/api/permalink/6d1d21f0–4649–4595-a0a1–5303e6a790cd/?context=1516831 (accessed July 13, 2018).

Review of *Circle K Cycles,* by Karen Tei Yamashita. *Publisher's Weekly,* April 23, 2001: 51.

Review of *Letters to Memory,* by Karen Tei Yamashita. *Kirkus Reviews,* June 27, 2017. https://advance-lexis-com.ezproxy.bgsu.edu:9443/api/permalink/5cc36c09–7d79–42c7–9fe7-a10186d63ef6/?context=1516831 (accessed June 4, 2018).

Review of *Letters to Memory,* by Karen Tei Yamashita. *New Pages,* July 5, 2017. https://www.newpages.com/book-reviews/letters-to-memory (accessed June 4, 2017).

Review of *Letters to Memory,* by Karen Tei Yamashita. *Publishers Weekly,* July 24, 2017. https://www.publishersweekly.com/978–1–56689–487–6 (accessed June 4, 2018).

Segal, Lewis. "Performance Art Review: 'Hannah Kusoh' Revue at Japan America Plaza Gallery." *Los Angeles Times,* September 11, 1989: Calendar, Part 6, page 4. https://search.proquest.com/docview/280877845?accountid=26417 (accessed July 21, 2018).

Straight, Susan. "Susan Straight on the Powerful Connection between Memory, Photos and the Stories We Tell." *Los Angeles Times,* January 18, 2018. http://www.latimes.com/books/jacketcopy/la-ca-jc-susan-straight-20180118-story.html (accessed June 4, 2018).

Williams, Sarah T. "Blending and Bending the Borders." *Minneapolis Star-Tribune,* March 13, 2005: F15.

Zisler, Michael. Review of *I Hotel. Boomcalifornia.com* 1.4 (2011): 76–79.

ARTICLES AND MONOGRAPHS

Adams, Rachel. "The Ends of America, the Ends of Postmodernism," *Twentieth Century Literature* 53.3 (2007): 248–72. https://www-jstor-org.ezproxy.bgsu.edu:9443/stable/20479813 (accessed November 16, 2017).

Arias, Luis. "NAFTA: The Good, the Bad, and the Ugly." *The Hispanic Outlook in Higher Education*, June 20, 2005: 30. https://search.proquest.com/docview/219245570?accountid=26417 (accessed March 22, 2018).

Bahng, Aimee. "Extrapolating Transnational Arcs, Excavating Imperial Legacies: The Speculative Acts of Karen Tei Yamashita's *Through the Arc of the Rain Forest*." *MELUS* 33. 4 (2008): 123–44. https://www-jstor-org.ezproxy.bgsu.edu:9443/stable/20343510 (accessed November 16, 2017).

Baird, Bruce. "Butoh: Dance of Darkness and Light." In *A History of Japanese Theatre*, edited by Jonah Salz, 321–25. Cambridge: Cambridge University Press, 2016.

Birns, Nicholas. "An Incomplete Journey: Settlement and Power in *Brazil-Maru*." In *Karen Tei Yamashita: Fictions of Magic and Memory*, edited by A. Robert Lee, 59–72. Honolulu: University of Hawai'i Press, 2018.

Chae, Youngsuk. *Politicizing Asian American Literature: Towards a Critical Multiculturalism*. New York: Routledge, 2008.

Cheung, King-Kok. "Re-Viewing Asian American Literary Studies." In *An Interethnic Companion to Asian American Literature*, edited by King-Kok Cheung, 1–38. Cambridge: Cambridge University Press, 1997.

Chong, Sylvia Shin Huey. "'Look, an Asian!': The Politics of Racial Interpellation in the Wake of the Virginia Tech Shootings." *Journal of Asian American Studies* 11.1 (2008): 27–60. doi:10.1353/jaas.2008.0007 (accessed July 21, 2018).

Chuh, Kandice. "Of Hemispheres and Other Spheres: Navigating Karen Tei Yamashita's Literary World." *American Literary History* 18.3 (2006): 618–37. muse.jhu.edu/article/202145 (accessed November 16, 2017).

Crawford, Chiyo. "From Desert Dust to City Soot: Environmental Justice and Japanese American Internment in Karen Tei Yamashita's *Tropic of Orange*." *MELUS* 38.3 (2013): 86–106. https://www-jstor-org.ezproxy.bgsu.edu:9443/stable/42001240 (accessed November 16, 2017).

Dong, Harvey. "Third World Liberation Comes to San Francisco State and UC Berkeley." In "Seizing the Moment: Twentieth-Century Chinese American Activism," supplement, *Chinese America: History & Perspectives–The Journal of the Chinese Historical Society of America* (2009): 95–106. https://search.proquest.com/docview/207440100?accountid=26417 (accessed July 21, 2018).

Eng, Chris A. "Queer Genealogies of (Be)Longing: On the Thens and Theres of Asian America in Karen Tei Yamashita's *I Hotel*." *Journal of Asian American Studies* 20.3 (2017): 345–72.

Entin, Joseph. "Globalization, Migration, and Contemporary Working-Class Literature." In *A History of American Working-Class Literature*, edited by Nicholas Coles and Paul Lauter, 376–91. Cambridge: Cambridge University Press, 2017.

Heise, Ursula K. "Local Rock and Global Plastic: World Ecology and the Experience of Place." *Comparative Literature Studies* 41.1 (2004): 126–52. https://www-jstor-org.ezproxy.bgsu.edu:9443/stable/40468106 (accessed December 10, 2017).

Hsu, Ruth Y. "The Cartography of Justice and Truthful Refraction Found in Karen Tei Yamashita's *Tropic of Orange*." In *Transnational Asian American Literature: Sites and Transits,* edited by Shirley Geok-lin Lim, John Blair Gamber, Stephen Hong Sohn, and Gina Valentino, 75–99. Philadelphia: Temple University Press, 2006.

Hsu, Ruth Y. "Karen Tei Yamashita's *Tropic of Orange* and Chaos Theory: Angels and a Motley Crew." In *Karen Tei Yamshita: Fictions of Magic and Memory,* edited by A. Robert Lee, 105–22. Honolulu: University of Hawai'i Press, 2018.

Hsu, Ruth Y. and Pamela Thoma, eds. *Approaches to Teaching the Works of Karen Tei Yamashita*. New York: MLA, 2020.

Iezzi, Julie A. "Kabuki: Superheroes and Femmes Fatales." In *A History of Japanese Theatre,* edited by Jonah Salz, 102–40. Cambridge: Cambridge University Press, 2016.

"Investors Shaking Threads in Urban Spider Web." *Oakland Post,* August 29, 1978: 1. https://search.proquest.com/docview/371739125?accountid=26417 (accessed March 29, 2018).

Jacobson, J. "Alumni Profile: Karen Tei Yamashita ('73)." *The Second Laird Miscellany: The Blog of the Carleton College English Department*. Carleton College, September 24, 2017. http://blogs.carleton.edu/englishdepartment/2017/09/24/alumni-profile-karen-tei-yamashita-73/ (accessed October 25, 2017).

Jin, Wen. "Inconspicuous Magic: Cognitive Theories of Narrative Influence and Karen Tei Yamashita's *I-Hotel*." *Journal of Narrative Theory* 45.3 (2015): 447–69.

Kagaya, Shinko, and Miura Hiroko. "Noh and Muromachi Culture." In *A History of Japanese Theatre,* edited by Jonah Salz, 24–61. Cambridge: Cambridge University Press, 2016.

Kakutani, Michiko. "I Know What Incarceration Does to Families: It Happened to Mine," *New York Times,* July 13, 2018: n.p. https://www.nytimes.com/2018/07/13/opinion/when-america-incarcerated-my-family.html (accessed July 20, 2018).

Karpilow, Quentin, et al. "NAFTA: 20 Years of Costs to Communities and the Environment." *Huffington Post,* March 2014: 1–20. http://big.assets.huffingtonpost.com/NAFTAReport.pdf (accessed July 7, 2018).

Keneally, Meghan. "Donald Trump Cites These FDR Policies to Defend Muslim Ban." *ABC News,* December 8, 2015: n.p. https://abcnews.go.com/Politics/donald-trump-cites-fdr-policies-defend-muslim-ban/story?id=35648128 (accessed June 14, 2018).

Krstovic, Jelena. "Karen Tei Yamashita." *Contemporary Literary Criticism,* edited by Lawrence J. Trudeau, vol. 382 (2015): n.p. *Literature Resource Center,* http://link.galegroup.com/apps/doc/H1146630000/LitRC?u=bgsu_main&sid=LitRC&xid=od353512. (accessed June 11, 2018).

LaLonde, Chris, "Did You Hear the One about . . . ? Humor in *Through the Arc of the Rain Forest* and *Brazil Maru*." In *Karen Tei Yamashita: Fictions of Magic and Memory,* edited by A. Robert Lee, 90–104. Honolulu: University of Hawai'i Press, 2018.

Lee, A. Robert, "House of Memory: Imagining Karen Tei Yamashita's *I Hotel*." In *Karen Tei Yamashita: Fictions of Magic and Memory,* edited by A. Robert Lee, 143–54. Honolulu: [under Lee, A. Robert, ed.] University of Hawai'i Press, 2018.

Lee, A. Robert, editor. *Karen Tei Yamashita: Fictions of Magic and Memory.* Honolulu: University of Hawai'i Press, 2018.

Lee, A. Robert, "Shift of Scene: Re-Viewing *Anime Wong*." In *Karen Tei Yamashita: Fictions of Magic and Memory,* edited by A. Robert Lee, 155–62. Honolulu: University of Hawai'i Press, 2018.

Lee, Josephine. "East West Players and Asian American Theatre: A Retrospective."

Theatre Survey 57.2 (2016): 238–41. https://doi.org/10.1017/S0040557416000089 (accessed July 21, 2018).

Lee, Rachel. "Asian American Cultural Production in Asian-Pacific Perspective." *boundary 2* 26.2 (1999): 231–54. https://www-jstor-org.ezproxy.bgsu.edu:9443/stable/303801 (accessed December 10, 2017).

Lee, Sue-Im. "We Are Not the World: Global Village, Universalism, and Karen Tei Yamashita's *Tropic of Orange*." *Modern Fiction Studies* 52.3 (2007): 501–27. https://muse-jhu-edu.ezproxy.bgsu.edu:9443/article/223008 (accessed October 24, 2017).

Ling, Jiqui. "Forging a North-South Perspective: Nikkei Migration in Karen Tei Yamashita's Novels." *Amerasia Journal* 32.3 (2006): 1–22.

Ling, Jinqi. *Across Meridians: History and Figuration in Karen Tei Yamashita's Transnational Novels.* Palo Alto, Calif.: Stanford University Press, 2012.

Lowe, Lisa. *Immigrant Acts: On Asian American Cultural Politics.* Durham, N.C.: Duke University Press, 1996.

Lowe, Lisa. *The Intimacies of Four Continents.* Durham, N.C.: Duke University Press, 2015.

Magosaki, Rei. *Tricksters & Cosmopolitans: Cross-Cultural Collaborations in Asian American Literary Production.* New York: Fordham University Press, 2016.

McAuliff, Michael. "NAFTA Report Warns of Trade Deal Environmental Disasters." *Huffington Post,* March 12, 2014. https://www.huffingtonpost.com/2014/03/11/nafta-environment_n_4938556.html (accessed July 7, 2018).

Melamed, Jody. *Represent and Destroy: Rationalizing Violence in the New Racial Capitalism.* Minneapolis: University of Minnesota Press, 2011.

Mermann-Jozwiak, Elisabeth. "Yamashita's Post-National Spaces: 'It All Comes Together in Los Angeles.'" *Canadian Review of American Studies/Revue canadienne d'études américaines* 41.1 (2011): 1–24. http://muse.jhu.edu.ezproxy.bgsu.edu:8080/article/424090 (accessed October 25, 2017).

Morley, David, and Kevin Robins. "Techno-Orientalism: Japan Panic." *Spaces of Identity: Global Media, Electronic Landscapes, and Cultural Boundaries.* New York: Routledge, 1995. 147–73.

Murayama, Mizuho. "The Virgin Land Deforested: The Male-Centered Perspective of Utopianism in Karen Tei Yamashita's *Brazil-Maru*." *AALA Journal* 11 (2005): 101–7. ezproxy.bgsu.edu:8080/login?url=http://search.ebscohost.com/login.aspx?direct=true&db=mzh&AN=2008380089&site=ehost-live&scope=site (accessed May 24, 2018).

Palumbo-Liu, David. "Embedded Lives: The House of Fiction, the House of History." *Profession* (2011): 13–22. https://www-jstor-org.ezproxy.bgsu.edu:9443/stable/41714104 (accessed March 27, 2017).

Paul, Deanna, and Avi Selk. "How the Supreme Court Struck Down a WWII-Era Travesty When It Upheld Trump's Travel Ban," *Washington Post,* June 27, 2018: n.p. https://www.washingtonpost.com/news/retropolis/wp/2018/06/27/they-traded-one-injustice-for-another-how-the-supreme-court-struck-down-a-wwii-era-travesty-when-it-upheld-trumps-travel-ban/?utm_term=.f95e5a2b7b56 (accessed July 20, 2018).

Ragain, Nathan. "A Revolutionary Romance: Particularity and Universality in Karen Tei Yamashita's *I Hotel*." *MELUS,* 38.1 (2013): 137–54.

Ragain, Nathan. "(Re)Production Cycles: Labor and National Identity in *Circle K Cycles*." In *Karen Tei Yamashita: Fictions of Magic and Memory,* edited by A. Robert Lee, 123–42. Honolulu: University of Hawai'i Press, 2018.

Rody, Caroline. "Impossible Voices: Ethnic Postmodern Narration in Toni Morrison's *Jazz* and Karen Tei Yamashita's *Through the Arc of the Rain Forest*." *Contemporary Literature* 41.4 (2000): 618–41. https://www-jstor-org.ezproxy.bgsu.edu:9443/stable/1209005 (accessed November 16, 2017).

Rody, Caroline. "The Transnational Imagination: Karen Tei Yamashita's *Tropic of Orange*." In *Asian North American Identities: Beyond the Hyphen,* edited by Eleanor Ty and Donald C. Goellnicht, 130–48. Bloomington: Indiana University Press, 2004.

Santa Ana, Jeffrey. *Racial Feelings: Asian America in a Capitalist Culture of Emotion.* Philadelphia: Temple University Press, 2015.

Simal, Begoña, Jesús Benito, and Ana M. Manzanas. "Of a Magical Nature: The Environmental Unconscious." *Critical Approaches to Ethnic American Literature* 3 (2009): 193–237. ezproxy.bgsu.edu:8080/login?url=http://search.ebscohost.com/login.aspx?direct=true&db=lkh&AN=58841760&site=ehost-live&scope=site (accessed July 21, 2018).

Song, Min Hyoung. "Becoming Planetary." *The Twenty-First Century American Novel,* special issue of *American Literary History* 23.3 (2011): 555–73. http://muse.jhu.edu.ezproxy.bgsu.edu:8080/article/449335 (accessed November 16, 2017).

Song, Min Hyoung. *The Children of 1965: On Writing, and Not Writing, as an Asian American.* Durham, N.C.: Duke University Press, 2013.

Sohn, Stephen Hong. "Introduction: Alien/Asian: Imagining the Racialized Future." *MELUS* 33.4 (2008): 5–22. www.jstor.org/stable/20343505 (accessed July 21, 2018).

Sohn, Stephen Hong. "*Anime Wong:* A Critical Afterword." In *Anime Wong: Fictions of Performance,* by Karen Tei Yamashita, 357–85. Minneapolis: Coffeehouse Press, 2014.

Sotomayor, Sonia. Dissenting opinion. *Donald J. Trump, President of the United States, et al., Petitioners v. Hawai'i, et al.* no. 17–965, 26 June 2018, 1–28. Supreme Court of the United States, https://www.supremecourt.gov/opinions/17pdf/17–965_h315.pdf. (accessed July 20, 2018).

Sugano, Douglas. "Karen Tei Yamashita." In *Asian American Novelists: A Bio-Bibliographical Critical Sourcebook,* edited by Emmanuel S. Nelson, 403–8. Westport, Conn.: Greenwood, 2000.

Terazawa, Yukiko. "Collective Memory and Camera Images in Karen Tei Yamashita's *Brazil-Maru*." *AALA Journal* 11 (2005): 126–41.

Terazawa, Yukiko. "'Shifting the Pattern of History': Narration and Counter-Memory in Karen Tei Yamashita's Brazil-Maru." *Feminist Studies in English Literature* 13.2 (2005): 129–53.

Thoma, Pamela. "Traveling the Distances of Karen Tei Yamashita's Fiction: A Review Essay on Yamashita Scholarship and Transnational Studies." *Asian American Literature: Discourse & Pedagogies* 1.1 (2010): 6–15. ezproxy.bgsu.edu:8080/login?url=http://search.ebscohost.com/login.aspx?direct=true&db=lkh&AN=70093150&site=ehost-live&scope=site (accessed November 16, 2017).

Vint, Sherryl. "Orange County: Global Networks in *Tropic of Orange*." *Science Fiction Studies* 39.1 (2012): 401–14. https://www-jstor-org.ezproxy.bgsu.edu:9443/stable/10.5621/sciefictstud.39.3.0401 (accessed November 16, 2017).

Wallace, Molly. "Tropics of Globalization: Reading the New North America." *Symplokē: A Journal for the Intermingling of Literary, Cultural and Theoretical Scholarship* 9.1–2 (2001): 145–60. https://www-jstor-org.ezproxy.bgsu.edu:9443/stable/40550506 (accessed November 16, 2017).

Wallace, Molly. "'A Bizarre Ecology': The Nature of Denatured Nature." *Contemporary Literary Criticism,* edited by Lawrence J. Trudeau, vol. 382 (2015): n.p. *Literature Resource Center,* http://link.galegroup.com.ezproxy.bgsu.edu:8080/apps/doc/H1100119950/LitRC?u=bgsu_main&sid=LitRC&xid=050c3743 (accessed July 21, 2018).

Weiner, Rachel. "Roanoke Mayor David Bowers: Reject Refugees Like US Interned Japanese." *Washington Post,* November 18, 2015: n.p. https://www.washingtonpost.com/local/virginia-politics/roanoke-mayor-david-bowers-reject-refugees-like-us-interned-japanese/2015/11/18/971468 1a-8e34–11e5-acff-673ae92ddd2b_story.html?utm_term=.9b6612e59cbc (accessed June 14, 2018).

Wong, Lily. "Dwelling over China: Minor Transnationalisms in Karen Tei Yamashita's *I Hotel.*" *The Chinese Factor: Reorienting Global Imaginaries in American Studies,* special issue of *American Quarterly* 69.3 (2017): 719–40.

Wong, Sau-ling Cynthia. *Reading Asian American Literature: From Necessity to Extravagance.* Princeton, N.J.: Princeton University Press, 1993.

Yu, Lai Ying. "Capturing the Spirit: Teaching Karen Tei Yamashita's *I Hotel.*" *Asian American Literature: Discourses and Pedagogies* 5 (2014): 61–86.

INDEX